Classic
GERMAN
Cookbook

Classic

GERMAN
Cookbook

70 traditional recipes from Germany, Austria, Hungary and
the Czech Republic, shown step by step in 300 photographs

Lesley Chamberlain with Catherine Atkinson and Trish Davies

southwater

This edition is published by Southwater, an imprint of Anness Publishing Ltd
Hermes House, 88–89 Blackfriars Road, London SE1 8HA
tel. 020 7401 2077; fax 020 7633 9499
www.southwaterbooks.com; www.annesspublishing.com

If you like the images in this book and would like to investigate using them for publishing, promotions or
advertising, please visit our website www.practicalpictures.com for more information.

UK agent: The Manning Partnership Ltd;
tel. 01225 478444; fax 01225 478440; sales@manning-partnership.co.uk
UK distributor: Grantham Book Services Ltd;
tel. 01476 541080; fax 01476 541061; orders@gbs.tbs-ltd.co.uk
North American agent/distributor: National Book Network;
tel. 301 459 3366; fax 301 429 5746; www.nbnbooks.com
Australian agent/distributor: Pan Macmillan Australia;
tel. 1300 135 113; fax 1300 135 103; customer.service@macmillan.com.au
New Zealand agent/distributor: David Bateman Ltd;
tel. (09) 415 7664; fax (09) 415 8892

Publisher: Joanna Lorenz
Editor: Margaret Malone
Photography: Dave Jordan and Ian Garlick
Food for photography: Sara Lewis, assisted by Julie Beresford, and Clare Lewis,
assisted by Sascha Brodie
Styling: Marion McLornan and Shannon Beare
Illustrators: Angela Woods (artworks) and David Cook (map)
Picture credit: p7 Magnum Photos

ETHICAL TRADING POLICY
Because of our ongoing ecological investment programme, you, as our customer, can have the pleasure and reassurance of
knowing that a tree is being cultivated on your behalf to naturally replace the materials used to make the book you are
holding. For further information about this scheme, go to www.annesspublishing.com/trees

A CIP catalogue record for this book is available from the British Library.

Previously published as *From Stroganov to Strudel*

NOTES
Bracketed terms are intended for American readers.

For all recipes, quantities are given in both metric and imperial measures and, where appropriate, in standard cups and spoons.
Follow one set of measures, but not a mixture, because they are not interchangeable.

Standard spoon and cup measures are level. 1 tsp = 5ml, 1 tbsp = 15ml, 1 cup = 250ml/8fl oz.

Australian standard tablespoons are 20ml. Australian readers should use 3 tsp in place of 1 tbsp
for measuring small quantities.

American pints are 16fl oz/2 cups. American readers should use 20fl oz/2.5 cups in place of 1 pint
when measuring liquids.

Electric oven temperatures in this book are for conventional ovens. When using a fan oven, the temperature will probably need to be
reduced by about 10–20°C/20–40°F. Since ovens vary, you should check with your manufacturer's instruction book for guidance.

Medium (US large) eggs are used unless otherwise stated.

Main front cover image shows Veal Roast – for recipe, see page 32

CONTENTS

INTRODUCTION

The Central European countries of Germany, Austria, Hungary, the Czech Republic and Slovakia comprise a geographical region that extends southwards from the cold shores of the North and Baltic Seas to the warmer climes of the Balkan countries. The foods characteristic of this area thus reflect a wide range of influences, though is dominated by a robust style that is famous world-wide.

CULINARY IDENTITY

On the everyday level of eating and drinking, national tastes within Central Europe have tended to remain simple and relatively distinct. The wide availability of many typical ingredients, however, such as caraway seeds, cucumbers, dill, mustard, soured cream and cabbage, has naturally resulted in an overlap of cooking styles, and sometimes recipes of neighbouring countries may vary only slightly in ingredients or method.

Czech cooking, for example, is solid and satisfying and bland in flavour except for the use of marjoram. Pale rye bread is preferred, as are salads of potato and other cooked vegetables, often dressed with mayonnaise. Potatoes are also fried with bacon or simmered with sausage to make quickly prepared supper dishes. Versatile use is made of other root crops such as kohlrabi and celeriac. The best loved of all Czech dishes however, has to be the dumpling. Made of flour, semolina or potato, in all shapes and sizes, these are served in savoury soups and stews as well as dessert dishes.

In contrast with such mild flavours and hefty textures, Hungarian cooking can be quite fiery and is rich in Mediterranean-style vegetables. The sour flavours and pickles that are so characteristic of the rest of Eastern Europe are less often seen in Hungarian cooking. The abundance of wheat ensures plenty of robust white bread, in place of darker breads, and more use of home-made pasta.

HUNGARIAN FINESSE

In the best of Hungarian cooking, as in some German cuisine, the use of red and white wine in meat and fish dishes has produced a greater complexity and subtlety than in other Central European cuisines, establishing a dividing line between good Hungarian cooking and the more usual country-style fare of the region. Hungarian chefs also have different ways of cooking meat and fish with paprika, according to whether or not the finished dish is

Left: The following collection of recipes concentrates on the Central European countries, where hearty peasant traditions sit alongside the opulence of dishes that flourished during the period of the great Austro-Hungarian Hapsburg Empire.

Right: Fresh produce available in the markets ranges from root vegetables characteristic of northern Europe to tomatoes, courgettes and peppers, more typical of the warmer southern cuisines.

dry or whether it contains cream. Goulash itself is always a dish with plenty of sauce.

It appears that the development of such fine Hungarian cuisine and the adoption of a wide variety of ingredients, including tomatoes, onions and peppers, was a consequence of an important royal marriage in the 15th century. In 1475 King Matthias married the daughter of the King of Naples, who imported new ingredients and chefs to make life beyond Italy's borders bearable. From these early refinements, Hungarian cuisine has rarely looked back.

MEAT DISHES

A key ingredient of this region's cooking is pork. Although the world-famous Austrian schnitzel is usually made with veal, across Germany and the other Central European countries pork is more commonly eaten, either as fried breadcrumbed steaks or cooked with peppers. In the Czech Republic, it is also often served wrapped around an egg, ham and cheese filling. It is also often stewed as a variation on the classic Hungarian goulash.

Cured pork, or bacon, provides another important ingredient in Central European cooking, valued for its unique pervasive flavour. Czech and Hungarian cooks, for instance, use bacon fat to achieve the distinctive tastes of many soups and otherwise meat-free fare, including dishes of long-simmered red cabbage.

Pork is also the major ingredient of the region's sausages. Czech sausages and Hungarian salami are famous worldwide, and every German region has its distinctive *wurst*, or sausage.

Beef perhaps rivals pork in popularity only in those parts of Central Eastern Europe where the best cattle are raised. One such place is the central Hungarian plain, or *puszta*, the original home of goulash, which is named after the *gulyás* (cowherds) who invented the prototype dish. While today's tempting recipes for this classic dish make use of paprika, caraway, green peppers and tomatoes, the cowherds of past centuries simply added water to meat they had previously cooked with onions then dried in the sun.

Although it has no such romantic history, German beef cookery is also excellent: for instance, recipes for *sauerbraten*, beef marinated in vinegar, sugar and seasonings then braised, serve simply to show off high-quality beef at its best.

JEWISH HERITAGE

Much of Central and Eastern European cuisine is known to the West in the guise of Jewish cooking, dating from the time when many Jewish communities inhabited this part of Europe. Czech and traditional Jewish cooking, for instance, share a taste for goose and beef as well as for carp served in sweetish sauces. Jewish *gefilte fisch*, carp stuffed with pike, uses two of the classic fish of the region. Pancakes, beans and fried cakes of grated raw potato figure in both cuisines. The Jewish Sabbath dish of *cholent*, bean and barley stew, is simply a kosher variation of the pork versions of the dish found everywhere in Central Europe. By the same token, Jewish recipes for red cabbage dispense with bacon.

CAKES AND SWEET PASTRIES

The fine tradition of cakes and sweet pastries common to southern Germany, Austria and Hungary owes much to the bread and pastry cooks of 18th-century Vienna, who in turn were inspired by a mixture of French and Turkish influences. German, Austro-Hungarian and Jewish cakemakers of the past two and a half centuries have together created the greatest torten and strudels in the world, and the most civilized surroundings in which to eat them while drinking coffee.

While the range of cakes available is great, a good plain cake which straddles all borders is the *gugelhupf* or *kugelhupf*. This is leavened with yeast and traditionally baked in a Turk's head mould.

INGREDIENTS

VEGETABLES

Fresh red and green peppers of the large capsicum variety, tomatoes and courgettes, parsley and dill are among the abundant vegetables and fresh herbs you would expect to see in a Hungarian market. In addition to large onions for cooking, spring onions are used in salads and to garnish soups. The more unusual root crops in Germany and the Czech lands include kohlrabi, a relative of the cabbage family, and celeriac, a large knobby root vegetable, which can be used in soups or salads.

MEAT AND POULTRY

Fresh pork is most popular, with goose cooked for special occasions. Central European food is most famous, however, for its smoked and unsmoked pork sausage and bacon. Bacon teams particularly well with cabbage and caraway, and

Above left: capsicum, tomatoes, celeriac, onions and kohlrabi.

Above right: assorted German breads, including sour dough, pumperknickel, rye and poppy seed.

Right, clockwise from front left: smoked loin, Hungarian guylai, *pork medallion steaks, boned shoulder, pork ribs,* bauernbratwurst, regensburgers *and* frankfurters.

bacon fat is often used to enhance the flavour of soups and stews. As for sausages, from Germany through the Czech Republic to Slovakia and Hungary, these are eternally popular street food, eaten simply with mustard and a roll, and they double as quick meals in pubs and restaurants. The number of varieties available from shops and delicatessens, from the frankfurter style to juicy fat specimens, can easily overwhelm the uninitiated. The range of salami-style sausage, which in German is called *wurst,* is equally wide and delicious.

GRAINS

Central Europe is the home of *mehlspeisen,* dishes of noodles or dumplings, which can be either sweet or savoury and take the place of a main meal. Dumplings are made of flour and semolina and sometimes include potato. Good wholemeal white flour is essential for fine baking, and excellent white bread is produced alongside traditional pale rye bread.

HERBS, SPICES AND OTHER FLAVOURINGS

Paprika was introduced to daily Hungarian cooking by the Turks some time before the 17th century, but it took a long time before the upper classes adopted the habit. To make paprika powder, the fleshy parts of peppers are dried and powdered, with a proportion of their seeds. The result is graded according to piquancy, fineness and colour, with the colours varying from bright red to yellowish brown. "Sweet noble" paprika is darker and more piquant than the

Above, anticlockwise from left: apples, plums, cherries, hazelnuts and almonds

Left, from left to right: dried chillies, paprika and fresh and bottled chillies

duller, lighter, half-sweet paprika, which can give a good colour to a dish without making it unbearably hot. Many Hungarian dishes are begun by lightly frying an onion and sprinkling some paprika powder over it.

Caraway seed, which has a cooling and digestive effect, is widely used in cabbage dishes and with pork. The flowery, pungent taste of fresh marjoram, which retains its flavour uniquely well among herbs when dried, is a year-round favourite with Czech cooks. Mustard of a mild European variety is the essential accompaniment to the boiled sausages of Central East Europe.

In baking, honey, poppy seeds and cake spices, such as cinnamon, cloves and cardamom, are used to flavour traditional sweet biscuits and breads, including gingerbread and plaited buns.

Right, clockwise from left: fresh marjoram; plain, dill and wholegrain mustards; cardamom; cinnamon sticks; poppy seeds; caraway seeds and allspice.

FRUIT

The plums, apricots and cherries of Central Europe make outstanding jams and pie fillings. Apples are widely used and are delicious with braised red cabbage. Germany is one of the largest apple-growing countries in the world, and there is seemingly no limit to the guises in which apples can appear, from strudels and pancakes to cakes.

DAIRY PRODUCTS

Hungarian *lipto* cheese is a speciality ewe's milk cheese, and is the chief ingredient in *liptauer*, a spread made with butter, paprika, caraway and onion. Curd cheese is used in savoury and sweet cooking.

DRINKS

Czech beer from Pilsen is arguably the finest in the world. Whatever the country of origin, German lager-style beer is enjoyed throughout Central Eastern Europe and is sometimes used in cooking.

Modest white table wines are produced in Moravia and Slovakia, but the best wine comes from Hungary, from around Lake Balaton and a little further north in the prized Badacsonyi region, and also in the south in Villany, close to Croatia and Serbia. Hungary is also famous for its very sweet dessert wine called *tokai*, produced in a small area in the north of the country, straddling the border with Slovakia. It may be drunk at both the beginning and end of a meal, or added to consommé.

Each Central European country has its favourite brandy or what the Germans call schnapps. One well-known example is the Hungarian *palinka*, made out of apricots. *Slivowicz*, made from plums, is common everywhere. A Czech speciality is a sweetish herbal liqueur called *bekerovka*.

SOUPS AND STARTERS

*Soups are a favourite in this area, served either as a main meal or as a starter.
Hearty soups range from creamy dishes such as Czech Cauliflower Soup
accompanied by light dumplings, to the famous fruit soups of Hungary and
chunky soups of Germany, such as Lentil Soup containing sliced frankfurter.
Many Central European starters consist of sour vegetables, cold meats, fish and
cheese. Served hot or cold, tasty starters such as Potato Pancakes and
Herby Liver Pâté Pie are ideal as snacks to serve with drinks.*

Cream of Spinach Soup

Rich and smooth, Hungarian creamed soups are made with double or soured cream and sometimes egg yolk, too.

INGREDIENTS

Serves 4

500g/1¼lb fresh young spinach, well washed

1.2 litres/2 pints/5 cups salted water

2 onions, very finely chopped or minced

25g/1oz/2 tbsp butter

45ml/3 tbsp plain flour

250ml/8fl oz/1 cup double cream

salt and freshly ground black pepper

2 hard-boiled eggs, sliced, and 2 grilled rindless bacon rashers, crumbled, to garnish

1 Remove and discard any coarse stems from the spinach leaves. Bring the salted water to the boil in a large pan. Add the spinach and cook for 5–6 minutes. Strain the spinach and reserve the liquid.

2 Blend the spinach in a food processor or blender to a purée.

3 Fry the chopped or minced onions in the butter in a large pan until pale golden brown. Remove from the heat and sprinkle in the flour. Return to the heat and cook for a further 1–2 minutes to cook the flour.

4 Stir in the reserved spinach liquid and, once it is all incorporated into the soup, bring it back to the boil.

5 Cook until thick then stir in the spinach purée and double cream. Reheat and adjust the seasoning. Serve the soup in bowls garnished with extra pepper, the sliced eggs and sprinkled with the crumbled bacon pieces.

Fish Soup with Dumplings

This Czech soup takes little time to make compared with a meat-based one. Use a variety of whatever fish is available, such as perch, catfish, cod, snapper or carp. The basis of the dumplings is the same whether you use semolina or flour.

INGREDIENTS

Serves 4–8

3 rindless bacon rashers, diced
675g/1½ lb assorted fresh fish, skinned, boned and diced
15ml/1 tbsp paprika, plus extra to garnish
1.5 litres/2½ pints/6¼ cups fish stock or water
3 firm tomatoes, peeled and chopped
4 waxy potatoes, peeled and grated
5–10ml/1–2 tsp chopped fresh marjoram, plus extra to garnish

For the dumplings
75g/3oz/½ cup semolina or flour
1 egg, beaten
45ml/3 tbsp milk or water
generous pinch of salt
15ml/1 tbsp chopped fresh parsley

1 Dry fry the diced bacon in a large pan until pale golden brown, then add the pieces of assorted fish. Fry for 1–2 minutes, taking care not to break up the pieces of fish.

2 Sprinkle in the paprika, pour in the fish stock or water, bring to the boil and simmer for 10 minutes.

3 Stir the tomatoes, grated potato and marjoram into the pan. Cook for 10 minutes, stirring occasionally.

4 Meanwhile, make the dumplings by mixing all the ingredients together, then leave to stand, covered with clear film, for 5–10 minutes.

5 Drop spoonfuls into the soup and cook for 10 minutes. Serve hot, with a little marjoram and paprika.

Hungarian Sour Cherry Soup

Particularly popular in summer, this fruit soup is typical of Hungarian cooking. The recipe makes good use of the plump, sour cherries available locally. Fruit soups are thickened with flour, and a touch of salt is added to help bring out the flavour of this cold soup.

INGREDIENTS

Serves 4
15ml/1 tbsp plain flour
120ml/4fl oz/½ cup soured cream
generous pinch of salt
5ml/1 tsp caster sugar
225g/8oz/1½ cups fresh sour or
  morello cherries, stoned
900ml/1½ pints/3¾ cups water
50g/2oz/¼ cup sugar

1 Blend the flour with the soured cream; add the salt and caster sugar.

2 Cook the cherries in the water, with the sugar. Gently poach for about 10 minutes.

> — COOK'S TIP —
>
> The soup is best made with fresh sour or cooking cherries such as morello; the flavour is simply not the same when canned, frozen or bottled cherries are used.

3 Remove from the heat and set aside 30ml/2 tbsp of the cooking liquid as a garnish. Stir another 30ml/2 tbsp of the cherry liquid into the flour and soured cream mixture then pour this on to the cherries.

4 Return to the heat. Bring to the boil then simmer for 5–6 minutes.

5 Remove from the heat, cover with clear film and leave to cool. Add extra salt if necessary. Serve with a little cooking liquid swirled in.

Czech Pork Soup

Originally, this soup would have been made from half or quarter of a pig's head, but these days a shoulder of pork is a little easier to procure and just as tasty.

INGREDIENTS

Serves 4–6
350g/12oz lean shoulder of pork or
  tenderloin, cut into 1cm/½in cubes
1 large onion, finely sliced
115g/4oz/²/₃ cup carrots, finely diced
3 garlic cloves, crushed
1.5 litres/2½ pints/6¼ cups water or
  pork stock
10ml/2 tsp chopped fresh marjoram
60–90ml/4–6 tbsp freshly cooked
  pearl barley or long grain rice
salt and freshly ground black pepper

1 Put the pork cubes, onion, carrot and garlic in a large pan. Pour in the water or stock.

> — COOK'S TIP —
>
> For a more substantial soup, double the quantity of barley or rice.

2 Simmer for 1–1½ hours, or until the meat is just tender.

3 Skim, if necessary, before adding the marjoram. Season to taste. Simmer for a further 5–10 minutes.

4 Place the barley or rice in serving bowls then ladle over the soup.

Chicken and Vegetable Soup

Packed with vegetables and tender chicken, this soup makes a nutritious and tasty main meal.

INGREDIENTS

Serves 6

1 small or medium chicken, skinned and trimmed of fat
1.5 litres/2½ pints/6¼ cups water
25g/1oz/2 tbsp butter
1 onion, finely chopped
2 carrots, finely chopped
½ small celeriac, diced
½ small cauliflower, cut into florets
115g/4oz/1 cup fresh peas
115g/4oz/generous cup white long-grain rice
salt and freshly ground black pepper
15ml/1 tbsp chopped fresh flat leaf parsley, to garnish

1 Rinse the chicken well and pat dry with kitchen paper.

2 Put the chicken in a large pan with the water and season well. Bring to the boil, reduce the heat and simmer gently for 1–1½ hours, or until the chicken is just tender.

3 Remove the chicken from the pan. Cut off all the meat into thick strips and keep warm. Discard the chicken carcass; skim the stock, if necessary, and reserve.

4 In a large pan, heat the butter and fry the onion until pale golden brown, before adding the carrots and celeriac. Cook gently for a further 3–4 minutes.

5 Stir in the cauliflower and peas, then pour in the reserved chicken stock and bring slowly to the boil. Reduce the heat and leave to simmer for 10 minutes.

6 Add the rice and chicken strips to the pan. Season well to taste. Cook the soup for a further 20 minutes, or until the rice is cooked. Serve the soup garnished with the parsley, with country bread.

Vegetable and Caraway Soup

Soups form a major part of Czech cuisine and are served either as a first course or as a main meal in themselves. Czechs use a traditional array of root vegetables, dried beans, peas and lentils. Caraway seeds are added for a distinctive flavour.

INGREDIENTS

Serves 6

450g/1lb mixed dried pulses, such as peas, lentils, navy beans, soaked overnight
1.75 litres/3 pints/7½ cups water
75g/3oz/6 tbsp butter
350g/12oz/2 cups finely chopped mixed root vegetables, such as parsnips, onion, carrot
3 garlic cloves, finely chopped
50g/2oz/½ cup plain flour
30ml/2 tbsp caraway seeds, lightly crushed
150ml/¼ pint/⅔ cup double cream
salt and freshly ground black pepper
flat leaf parsley, to garnish

For the croûtons

2 bread slices, crusts removed, cut into 1cm/½ inch cubes
45ml/3 tbsp olive or vegetable oil

1 Drain the soaked dried pulses well and place in a large pan covered with the water. Simmer gently for 1½–2 hours, or until tender. Drain, reserving the cooking liquid.

2 Mash the cooked pulses or purée them in a food processor or blender. Return the purée to the pan along with the reserved cooking liquid.

3 In another pan melt the butter and fry the vegetables and garlic for 5 minutes, stirring all the time. Add the flour and the pulses purée and liquid. Season to taste. Bring to the boil and reduce the heat. Simmer for 20 minutes then add the caraway seeds.

4 Meanwhile, make the croûtons by frying the bread cubes in the oil until golden brown.

5 Remove the soup from the heat, stir in the cream and reheat. Adjust the seasoning and serve hot with the croûtons and sprinkled with the parsley.

Stuffed Mushrooms with Spinach

The large, flat, wild or cultivated mushrooms are excellent in this recipe, but use fresh ceps instead for perfection.

INGREDIENTS

Serves 6
12 large flat mushrooms
450g/1lb small young spinach leaves, well washed
3 rindless bacon rashers, cut into 5mm/¼in dice
1 onion, finely chopped
2 egg yolks, beaten
40g/1½oz/¾ cup fresh breadcrumbs
5ml/1 tsp chopped fresh marjoram
45ml/3 tbsp olive or vegetable oil
115g/4oz/1 cup feta cheese, crumbled
salt and freshly ground black pepper

1 Peel the mushrooms only if necessary. Remove the stalks and chop them finely.

2 Blanch the spinach by dropping into a pan of boiling water for 1–2 minutes, then plunge into cold water. Squeeze the spinach in kitchen paper, drying it thoroughly to prevent the filling being watery, then chop.

3 Dry fry the bacon rashers and chopped onion together in a pan until golden brown, then add the mushroom stalks. Remove from the heat. Stir in the spinach, egg yolks, breadcrumbs and marjoram and season to taste.

4 Place the mushrooms on a baking sheet and brush with a little oil.

5 Place heaped tablespoons of the spinach mixture on to the mushroom caps. Sprinkle over the cheese and cook the mushrooms under a preheated grill for about 10 minutes, or until golden brown.

Potato Pancakes

These little snacks are popular street food in the Czech Republic, and they are available at roadside stalls and cafés. Quick and easy to make, they are a tasty adaptation of the classic flour-based pancake.

INGREDIENTS

Serves 6–8
6 large waxy potatoes, peeled
2 eggs, beaten
1–2 garlic cloves, crushed
115g/4oz/1 cup plain flour
5ml/1 tsp chopped fresh marjoram
50g/2oz/4 tbsp butter
60ml/4 tbsp oil
salt and freshly ground black pepper
soured cream, chopped fresh parsley
    and a tomato salad, to serve

1 Grate the potatoes and squeeze thoroughly dry, using a dish towel.

2 Put the potatoes in a bowl with the eggs, garlic, flour, marjoram and seasoning and mix well.

3 Heat half the butter and oil together in a large frying pan then add large spoonfuls of the potato mixture to form rounds. Carefully flatten the "pancakes" well with the back of a dampened spoon.

--- COOK'S TIP ---

Put potatoes in water with a few drops of lemon, to prevent them turning brown.

4 Fry the pancakes until crisp and golden brown then turn over and cook on the other side. Drain on kitchen paper and keep warm while cooking the rest of the pancakes, adding the remaining butter and oil to the frying pan as necessary.

5 Serve the pancakes topped with soured cream, sprinkled with parsley, and accompanied by a fresh, juicy tomato salad.

Herby Liver Pâté Pie

A delicious luncheon dish with a glass of Pilsen beer.

INGREDIENTS

Serves 10
675g/1½lb minced pork
350g/12oz pork liver
350g/12oz/2 cups cooked ham, diced
1 small onion, finely chopped
30ml/2 tbsp chopped fresh parsley
5ml/1 tsp German mustard
30ml/2 tbsp Kirsch
5ml/1 tsp salt
beaten egg, for sealing and glazing
25g/1oz sachet aspic jelly
250ml/8fl oz/1 cup boiling water
freshly ground black pepper
bread and dill pickles, to serve

For the pastry
450g/1lb/4 cups plain flour
pinch of salt
275g/10oz/1¼ cups butter
2 eggs
1 egg yolk
30ml/2 tbsp water

1 Preheat the oven to 200°C/400°F/ Gas 6. To make the pastry, sift the flour and salt and rub in the butter. Beat the eggs, egg yolk and water, add to the dry ingredients and mix.

2 Knead the dough briefly until smooth. Roll out two-thirds on a lightly floured surface and use to line a 10 × 25cm/4 × 10in hinged loaf tin. Trim any excess dough.

3 Process half the pork and the liver until fairly smooth. Stir in the remaining minced pork, ham, onion, parsley, mustard, Kirsch and seasoning.

4 Spoon the filling into the tin, smoothing it down and levelling the surface.

5 Roll out the remaining pastry on the lightly floured surface and use it to top the pie, sealing the edges with some of the beaten egg. Decorate with the pastry trimmings and glaze with the remaining beaten egg. Using a fork, make 3 or 4 holes in the top, for the steam to escape.

6 Bake for 40 minutes, then reduce the oven temperature to 180°C/ 350°F/Gas 4 and cook for a further hour. Cover the pastry with foil if the top begins to brown too much. Allow the pie to cool in the tin.

7 Make up the aspic jelly, using the boiling water. Stir to dissolve, then allow to cool.

8 Make a small hole near the edge of the pie with a skewer, then pour in the aspic through a greaseproof paper funnel. Chill for at least 2 hours before serving the pie in slices with mustard, bread and dill pickles.

Vegetable Salad

This salad is a delicious blend of typical Central East European ingredients – soured cream, dill pickle, lemon juice and paprika. It is generally served as a starter alongside cold meats or poultry.

INGREDIENTS

Serves 6

225g/8oz/1½ cups green beans, trimmed
2 carrots, diced
115g/4oz/1 cup fresh or frozen peas
6 egg yolks
15ml/1 tbsp German mustard
30ml/2 tbsp granulated sugar
45ml/3 tbsp freshly squeezed lemon juice
400ml/14fl oz/1⅔ cups soured cream
1 small cooking apple, cored and diced
2–3 celery sticks, diced
1 dill pickle, diced
3 hard-boiled eggs
5ml/1 tsp chopped fresh parsley
30ml/2tbsp fresh breadcrumbs
5ml/1 tsp paprika
salt and freshly ground black pepper

1 Cook the green beans, carrots and peas in a large saucepan of boiling salted water for 5–8 minutes. Drain well then plunge into cold water to refresh. Drain well again.

2 Blend together in a heatproof bowl the egg yolks, mustard, sugar, lemon juice, soured cream and seasoning. Place the bowl containing the mixture over a pan of simmering water, stirring all the time until the sauce starts to thicken.

3 Remove from the heat and stir in the cooked vegetables, apple, celery and dill pickle. Mix well, then cover and chill.

4 Cut the hard-boiled eggs in half lengthways and carefully remove the yolks into a small mixing bowl, keeping the egg whites intact.

5 Blend the cooked egg yolks well with the parsley, breadcrumbs, paprika and a little seasoning. Use the filling to stuff the egg whites. Arrange the chilled vegetables on a serving plate and top with the stuffed eggs.

--- COOK'S TIP ---

If German mustard is too strong, replace with either a grainy mustard or chopped fresh tarragon.

MEAT AND POULTRY

*Lamb, beef, veal and chicken are all used in Central European cooking,
though it is perhaps pork that best exemplifies German and Central
European meat cooking. Roasts feature often, as do casseroles and stews, which
are often served with dumplings. The sweet-sour flavour so typical across this
region is again in evidence with sauces and meat stews containing dill pickles
and sauerkraut. In Hungary, however, the presence of paprika, introduced from
Turkey, has led to many classic dishes, of which Goulash is just one.*

Leg of Lamb with Pickle Sauce

Lamb is generally reserved for special occasions and festivals in Hungary. The sourness of the pickle sauce is an unusual contrast to the rich lamb.

INGREDIENTS

Serves 6–8

1.75kg/4lb lean leg of lamb
30–45ml/2–3 tbsp granular salt
finely grated rind of 1 lemon
50g/2oz/4 tbsp butter
4 rosemary sprigs
handful of flat leaf parsley
extra sprigs of rosemary and flat
   leaf parsley, to garnish
braised red cabbage,
   to serve

For the pickle sauce

8–10 gherkins
25g/1oz/2 tbsp butter
50g/2oz/½ cup flour
250ml/8fl oz/1 cup lamb stock
generous pinch of saffron
30ml/2 tbsp soured cream
5–10ml/1–2 tsp white wine vinegar
salt and freshly ground black pepper

1 Preheat the oven to 180°C/350°F/ Gas 4. Flatten the lamb with a rolling pin, rub with salt; leave for 30 minutes.

2 Mix together the lemon rind and butter. Place the lamb in a roasting tin and spread the lemon butter over.

3 Add the fresh herbs to the tin and roast for 1½–1¾ hours, basting occasionally. Strain the meat juices.

4 Meanwhile, make the pickle sauce. Process the gherkins coarsely. Heat the butter in a small pan and cook the gherkins for 5 minutes, stirring occasionally. Remove from the heat. Sprinkle in the flour and stir for a further 2–3 minutes.

5 Slowly pour the stock into the pan and bring to the boil. Stir in the saffron. Allow the sauce to simmer for a further 15 minutes.

6 Off the heat stir in the soured cream, vinegar and the strained meat juices. Season to taste. Garnish with herbs and serve with the sauce and red cabbage.

COOK'S TIP

Let the lamb stand for 10–20 minutes after cooking to allow the fibres in the meat to relax, making it more tender, firmer and easier to carve.

Lamb Goulash with Tomatoes and Peppers

Goulash is a dish that has travelled across Europe from Hungary and is popular in many places such as the Czech Republic and Germany. This Czech recipe is not a true goulash, however, because of the addition of flour. Nevertheless, it has a wonderful infusion of tomatoes, paprika, green peppers and marjoram.

INGREDIENTS

Serves 4–6

30ml/2 tbsp vegetable oil or melted lard (optional)
900g/2lb lean lamb, trimmed and cut into cubes
1 large onion, roughly chopped
2 garlic cloves, crushed
3 green peppers, seeded and diced
30ml/2 tbsp paprika
2 × 397g/14oz cans chopped plum tomatoes
15ml/1tbsp chopped fresh flat leaf parsley
5ml/1 tsp chopped fresh marjoram
30ml/2 tbsp plain flour
60ml/4 tbsp cold water
salt and freshly ground black pepper
green salad, to serve

1 Heat up the oil or lard, if using, in a frying pan. Dry fry or fry the pieces of lamb for 5–8 minutes, or until browned on all sides. Season well.

2 Add the onion and garlic and cook for a further 2 minutes before adding the green peppers and paprika.

3 Pour in the tomatoes and enough water, if needed, to cover the meat in the pan. Stir in the herbs. Bring to the boil, turn down the heat, cover and simmer very gently for 1½ hours, or until the lamb is tender.

4 Blend the flour with the cold water and pour into the stew. Bring back to the boil then reduce the heat to a simmer and cook until the sauce has thickened. Adjust the seasoning and serve the lamb goulash with a crisp green salad.

Loin of Pork with Prune Stuffing

Pork is by far the most popular meat in Germany and appears in many guises. Crushed ginger biscuits are a traditional thickening ingredient and add colour and flavour to a sauce.

INGREDIENTS

Serves 4

1.5kg/3lb cured or smoked loin of pork
75g/3oz/about 18 ready-to-eat prunes, finely chopped
45ml/3 tbsp apple juice or water
75g/3oz/1½ cups day-old ginger biscuit crumbs
3 cardamom pods
15ml/1 tbsp sunflower oil
1 onion, chopped
250ml/8fl oz/1 cup dry red wine
15ml/1 tbsp soft dark brown sugar
salt and freshly ground black pepper
buttery fried stoned prunes and apple and leek slices with steamed green cabbage, to serve

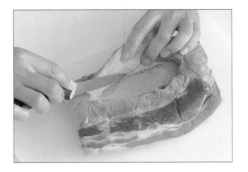

1 Preheat the oven to 230°C/450°F/ Gas 8. Put the pork, fat side down on a board. Make a cut about 3cm/ 1¼in deep along the length to within 1cm/½in of the ends, then make 2 deep cuts to its left and right, to create 2 pockets in the meat.

2 Put the prunes in a bowl. Spoon over the apple juice or water, then add the biscuit crumbs. Remove the cardamom seeds from their pods and crush using a pestle and mortar, or on a board with the end of a rolling pin. Add to the bowl with salt and pepper.

3 Mix the prune stuffing well and use to fill the pockets in the meat.

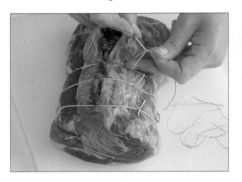

4 Tie the pork joint at regular intervals with string. Heat the oil in a roasting tin set on the hob and brown the joint over a high heat. Remove the meat and set aside.

5 Add the chopped onion to the tin and fry for 10 minutes, until golden. Return the pork to the tin, pour in the wine and add the sugar and seasoning.

6 Roast for 10 minutes, then reduce the oven temperature to 180°C/ 350°F/Gas 4 and roast, uncovered, for a further 1 hour and 50 minutes, or until cooked and golden brown.

7 Remove the joint from the tin and keep warm. Strain the meat juices through a sieve into a pan and simmer for 10 minutes, until slightly reduced. Carve the pork and serve with the sauce separately, accompanied by buttery fried stoned prunes and apple and leek slices, together with steamed green cabbage.

Braised Spicy Spare Ribs

Choose really meaty ribs for this dish and trim off any excess fat before cooking, as the juices are turned into a delicious sauce.

INGREDIENTS

Serves 6

25g/1oz/¼ cup plain flour
5ml/1 tsp salt
5ml/1 tsp ground black pepper
1.5kg/3½lb pork spare ribs, cut into
    individual pieces
30ml/2 tbsp sunflower oil
1 onion, finely chopped
1 garlic clove, crushed
45ml/3 tbsp tomato purée
30ml/2 tbsp chilli sauce
30ml/2 tbsp red wine vinegar
pinch of ground cloves
600ml/1 pint/2½ cups beef stock
15ml/1 tbsp cornflour
flat leaf parsley, to garnish
sauerkraut and crusty bread, to serve

1 Preheat the oven to 180°C/350°F/ Gas 4. Combine the flour, salt and black pepper in a shallow dish. Add the ribs and toss to coat them in flour.

2 Heat the oil in a large frying pan and cook the ribs, turning them until well browned. Transfer them to a roasting tin and sprinkle over the chopped onion.

COOK'S TIP

If time allows, first marinate the ribs in sunflower oil mixed with red wine vinegar.

3 In a bowl, mix together the garlic, tomato purée, chilli sauce, vinegar, cloves and stock. Pour over the ribs, then cover with foil. Roast for 1½ hours, or until tender, removing the foil for the last 30 minutes.

4 Tip the juices from the roasting tin into a small pan. Blend the cornflour in a cup with a little cold water and stir in. Bring the sauce to the boil, stirring, then simmer for 2–3 minutes until thickened.

5 Arrange the ribs on a bed of sauerkraut, then pour over a little sauce. Serve the remaining sauce separately in a warmed jug. Garnish with flat leaf parsley and serve with sauerkraut and crusty bread.

Pork Stew with Sauerkraut

An excellent combination of classic Central European flavours.

INGREDIENTS

Serves 4–6
30ml/2 tbsp vegetable oil or lard
2 onions, finely chopped
2 garlic cloves, crushed
900g/2lb lean pork, cut into 5cm/
    2in cubes
5ml/1 tsp caraway seeds (optional)
15ml/1 tbsp chopped fresh dill
900ml/1½ pints/3¾ cups warm pork
    or vegetable stock
900g/2lb/4 cups sauerkraut, drained
15ml/1 tbsp paprika
salt
dill, to garnish
soured cream, sprinkled with paprika,
    and pickled chillies (optional),
    to serve

1 Heat the oil or lard in a large pan and cook the onion and crushed garlic cloves until soft.

2 Add the pork cubes to the pan and fry until browned. Stir in the caraway seeds, if using, and fresh dill and pour in the stock. Cook for 1 hour over a gentle heat.

3 Stir the drained sauerkraut into the pork with the paprika. Leave to simmer gently for 45 minutes. Add salt, to taste.

4 Garnish the stew with a little more dill and serve with soured cream sprinkled with paprika, with pickled chillies, if liked.

Pork and Garlic Sausage Casserole

This hearty and filling casserole contains a variety of pork cuts. The light ale helps tenderize and flavour the meat.

INGREDIENTS

Serves 6
45ml/3 tbsp sunflower oil
225g/8oz lean, smoked bacon, rinded
    and diced
450g/1lb lean shoulder of pork,
    trimmed and cut into 2.5cm/
    1in cubes
1 large onion, sliced
900g/2lb potatoes, thickly sliced
250ml/8fl oz/1 cup light ale
225g/8oz/2 cups German garlic
    sausage, skinned and sliced
500g/1¼lb/2¼ cups sauerkraut,
    drained
2 red eating apples, cored and sliced
5ml/1 tsp caraway seeds
salt and freshly ground black pepper

1 Preheat the oven to 180°C/350°F/ Gas 4. Heat 30ml/2 tbsp of the oil in a flameproof casserole. Fry the bacon for 2–3 minutes, then lightly brown the cubes of pork. Set aside.

2 Add the remaining oil to the pan and gently cook the onion for 10 minutes, until soft. Return the meat to the pan and add the potatoes.

3 Stir in the ale and bring to the boil. Cover and cook for 45 minutes.

4 Stir in the garlic sausage, drained sauerkraut, sliced apple and caraway seeds. Season with salt and pepper. Return to the oven and cook the casserole for a further 30 minutes, or until the meat is tender.

Veal Roast

Veal is often flattened then layered or rolled around fillings. This mixture of veal, bacon, egg and ham as a filling is delicious.

INGREDIENTS

Serves 4–6

1.5kg/3lb shoulder of veal or lean pork, cut into 2cm/³/₄in slices
225g/8oz smoked bacon rashers
175g/6oz sliced ham
4 eggs, beaten
45ml/3 tbsp milk
3 dill pickles, finely diced
115g/4oz/¹/₂ cup butter
45ml/3 tbsp plain flour
350ml/12fl oz/1¹/₂ cups water or chicken stock
salt and freshly ground black pepper
baby carrots, runner beans and dill pickle slices, to serve

1 Preheat the oven to 180°C/350°F/ Gas 4. Place the veal or pork between 2 pieces of clear film and pound or flatten into a regular shape using a meat mallet or rolling pin.

2 Top each slice of veal or pork with a layer of bacon and ham. Beat the eggs in a small pan with the milk and stir until the mixture is softly scrambled. Leave to cool a little.

3 Place a layer of the scrambled egg on top of each slice and spread with a knife, then sprinkle on the finely diced dill pickle.

4 Carefully roll up each slice like a Swiss roll. Tie the rolls securely at regular intervals with string.

5 Heat the butter in a large flameproof casserole. Add the meat rolls and brown on all sides. Remove the pan from the heat. Remove the rolls and set aside. Sprinkle the flour into the pan and stir well.

6 Return the pan to the heat and cook the flour mixture until pale brown then slowly add half of the water. Return the meat rolls to the pan and bring to the boil, then put the casserole in the oven for 1³/₄–2 hours to roast slowly, adding the remaining water during cooking if necessary to prevent the veal from drying out.

7 When cooked, leave the rolls to stand for 10 minutes, before serving in slices with the gravy and baby carrots, runner beans and dill pickle.

Hungarian Goulash

Paprika is a distinctive feature of Hungarian cookery. It is a spicy seasoning ground from a variety of sweet red pepper, which has been grown in this area since the end of the 16th century. Shepherds added the spice to their *gulyás*, and fishermen used it in their stews.

INGREDIENTS

Serves 4–6
30ml/2 tbsp vegetable oil or
   melted lard
2 onions, chopped
900g/2lb braising or stewing steak,
   trimmed and cubed
1 garlic clove, crushed
generous pinch of caraway seeds
30ml/2 tbsp paprika
1 firm ripe tomato, chopped
2.4 litres/4 pints/10 cups beef stock
2 green peppers, seeded and sliced
450g/1lb potatoes, diced
salt

For the dumplings
2 eggs, beaten
90ml/6 tbsp plain flour, sifted

1 Heat the oil or lard in a large heavy-based pan. Add the onion and cook until soft.

2 Add the beef cubes to the pan and cook for 10 minutes browning gently, stirring frequently to prevent the meat from sticking.

3 Add the garlic, caraway seeds and a little salt to the pan. Remove from the heat and stir in the paprika and tomato. Pour in the beef stock and cook, covered, over a gentle heat for 1–1½ hours, or until tender.

4 Add the peppers and potatoes to the pan and cook for a further 20–25 minutes stirring occasionally.

5 Meanwhile, make the dumplings by mixing the beaten eggs together with the flour and a little salt. With lightly floured hands roll out the dumplings and drop them into the simmering stew for about 2–3 minutes, or until they rise to the surface of the stew. Adjust the seasoning and serve the goulash in warm dishes.

Roast Beef Marinated in Vegetables

This classic Czech dish uses only the best ingredients, including fillet of beef. You could use a sirloin instead, but you should allow a little extra cooking time.

INGREDIENTS

Serves 6

900g/2lb fillet or sirloin
2 rindless bacon rashers, finely shredded
2 onions, finely chopped
2 carrots, finely chopped
2 parsnips, finely chopped
225g/8oz/1 cup celeriac or 4 celery sticks, finely diced
2 bay leaves
2.5ml/¹/₂ tsp allspice
5ml/1 tsp dried thyme
30ml/2 tbsp chopped fresh flat leaf parsley
250ml/8 fl oz/1 cup red wine vinegar
60ml/4 tbsp olive oil
50g/2oz/4 tbsp butter
2.5ml/¹/₂ tsp sugar
salt and freshly ground black pepper
120ml/4fl oz/¹/₂ cup soured cream
flat leaf parsley, to garnish

For the dumplings
6 large potatoes, peeled and quartered
115g/4oz/1 cup plain flour
2 eggs, beaten

1 The day before, lard the beef with strips of bacon and season well.

2 Place the beef in a non-metallic bowl and sprinkle around the vegetables and bay leaves.

3 In another bowl mix together the allspice, thyme, parsley, vinegar and half of the olive oil. Pour this over the beef. Cover with clear film and place in the refrigerator. Leave for 2–3 hours, or longer if possible. Baste the beef occasionally with the marinade.

4 Preheat the oven to 180°C/350°F/Gas 4. Heat the remaining olive oil in a pan, add the beef and brown all over. Transfer the joint to a large roasting tin. Pour a little water into the pan to de-glaze, stir well, then pour over the meat.

5 Spoon the vegetable marinade around the joint in the roasting tin and dot the top of the meat with the butter. Sprinkle on the sugar. Roast for 1¹/₄–1¹/₂ hours, basting occasionally.

> ——— COOK'S TIP ———
>
> Larding means to insert thins strips of pork or bacon, called lardons, into a cut of meat. This is done to ensure that the cooked meat is moist and tender. Insert the strips with a larding needle or use your fingers.

6 Meanwhile, make the dumplings. Cook the potatoes for 15–20 minutes, drain then mash well. Sprinkle the flour over the potatoes with half the egg and stir well. When all the flour is incorporated add the remaining egg.

7 Turn the potato mixture on to a lightly floured surface and shape into 2 evenly sized oblongs. Bring a pan of salted water to the boil and cook for about 20 minutes. Leave to cool a little before slicing into portions.

8 While the dumplings are cooking remove the joint from the roasting tin and leave to stand before carving. Remove a spoonful of the cooked vegetables and reserve for garnishing. Carefully purée the remaining vegetables and meat juices in a food processor or blender.

9 Reheat the vegetable purée in a pan and season to taste. Add a little extra water if the sauce is too thick. Stir in the soured cream. Serve the beef in slices with the sauce and dumplings and garnish with reserved vegetables and parsley sprigs.

Czech Meatloaf

This is a satisfying meatloaf, popular with all the family.

INGREDIENTS

Serves 6–8
25g/2 tbsp butter
3 rindless bacon rashers, finely chopped
1 large onion, chopped
2 garlic cloves, crushed
450g/1lb lean minced pork
450g/1lb lean minced beef
75g/3oz fresh breadcrumbs
50ml/2fl oz/¼ cup milk
5ml/1 tsp chopped fresh thyme
30ml/2 tbsp chopped fresh flat leaf parsley
2 eggs, beaten
salt and freshly ground black pepper
roast potatoes and spinach, to serve

1 Preheat the oven to 180°C/350°F/ Gas 4. Grease and line a deep 20cm/8in square cake tin with greaseproof paper. Heat the butter in a pan and fry the bacon for 2–3 minutes, before adding the onion and garlic. Cook for another 2–3 minutes.

2 Mix all the remaining ingredients with the bacon mixture in a bowl, ensuring the meat breaks up completely.

3 Spoon the meat mixture into the prepared tin. Smooth the surface with a round-bladed knife.

4 Cover the tin with foil and bake for 1½ hours. Serve the loaf hot in thick slices with roasted potatoes and freshly cooked spinach.

Rabbit with Mustard Sauce

The delicate flavour of rabbit is enhanced here by the combined sharpness of the mustard, garlic and capers.

INGREDIENTS

Serves 4
45ml/3 tbsp vegetable oil or melted lard
1 rabbit, cut into joints
1 large onion, chopped
1 large garlic clove, crushed
350ml/12fl oz/1½ cups dry white wine
30ml/2 tbsp bottled capers, drained
30ml/2 tbsp chopped fresh flat leaf parsley
10ml/2 tsp chopped fresh marjoram
30–45ml/2–3 tbsp Dijon or German mustard
salt and freshly ground black pepper
flat leaf parsley, to garnish
freshly cooked carrots, to serve

1 Heat the vegetable oil or lard in a large flameproof casserole. Brown the pieces of rabbit before stirring in the onion. Sauté the onion for 2–3 minutes or until pale golden in colour.

--- COOK'S TIP ---

An authentic wine for this recipe would be from Moravia, the main Czech wine-producing area. Moravia produces light and flowery modest white table wines.

2 Stir the garlic into the casserole and pour in the white wine, drained capers, fresh herbs and mustard. Bring to the boil, then reduce the heat to a simmer. Season to taste.

3 Cover the pan and cook for 45–60 minutes, until tender. Garnish the rabbit with flat leaf parsley and serve with freshly cooked carrots.

Sauerbraten

The classic sweet-sour marinade gives this dish its name.

INGREDIENTS

Serves 6
1kg/2¼lb silverside of beef
30ml/2 tbsp sunflower oil
1 onion, sliced
115g/4oz smoked streaky bacon, diced
15ml/1 tbsp cornflour
50g/2oz/1 cup crushed ginger biscuits
flat leaf parsley, to garnish
buttered noodles, to serve

For the marinade
2 onions, sliced
1 carrot, sliced
2 celery sticks, sliced
600ml/1 pint/2½ cups water
150ml/¼ pint/⅔ cup red vinegar
1 bay leaf
6 cloves
6 whole black peppercorns
15ml/1 tbsp soft dark brown sugar
10ml/2 tsp salt

1 To make the marinade, put the onions, carrot and celery into a pan with the water. Bring to the boil and simmer for 5 minutes. Add the remaining marinade ingredients and simmer for a further 5 minutes. Cover and leave to cool.

2 Put the joint in a casserole into which it just fits. Pour over the marinade, cover and leave to marinate in the refrigerator for 3 days if possible, turning the joint daily.

3 Remove the joint from the marinade and dry thoroughly using kitchen paper. Heat the oil in a large frying pan and brown the beef over a high heat. Remove the joint and set aside. Add the sliced onion to the pan and fry for 5 minutes. Add the bacon and cook for a further 5 minutes, or until lightly browned.

4 Strain the marinade, reserving the liquid. Put the onion and bacon in a large flameproof casserole or pan, then put the beef on top. Pour over the marinade liquid. Slowly bring to the boil, cover, then simmer over a low heat for 1½–2 hours, or until the beef is very tender.

5 Remove the beef and keep warm. Blend the cornflour in a cup with a little cold water. Add to the cooking liquid with the ginger biscuit crumbs and bring to the boil, stirring. Thickly slice the beef and serve on a bed of hot buttered noodles. Garnish with sprigs of fresh flat leaf parsley and serve the gravy separately.

Chicken with Wild Mushrooms and Garlic

This roasted chicken dish has a hint of fresh herbs.

INGREDIENTS

Serves 4

45ml/3 tbsp olive or vegetable oil
1.5kg/3lb chicken
1 large onion, finely chopped
3 celery sticks, chopped
2 garlic cloves, crushed
275g/10oz/4 cups fresh wild
   mushrooms, sliced if large
5ml/1 tsp chopped fresh thyme
250ml/8fl oz/1 cup chicken stock
250ml/8fl oz/1 cup dry white wine
juice of 1 lemon
30ml/2 tbsp chopped fresh parsley
120ml/4fl oz/½ cup soured cream
salt and freshly ground black pepper
flat leaf parsley, to garnish
fresh green beans, to serve

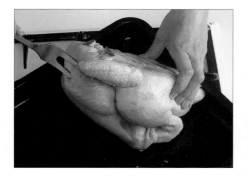

1 Preheat the oven to 190°C/375°F/ Gas 5. Heat the oil in a roasting tin and brown the chicken all over.

2 Add the onion and fry for about 2 minutes. Add the next 4 ingredients and cook for 3 minutes.

3 Pour the chicken stock, wine and lemon juice into the roasting tin. Sprinkle over half of the parsley and season well. Place the chicken in the oven and cook for 1½–1¾ hours, or until tender, basting occasionally to prevent drying out.

COOK'S TIP

Clean wild mushrooms well to remove any grit, or use cultured mushrooms instead.

4 Remove the chicken from the roasting tin and keep warm. Put the roasting tin on the hob and stir in the soured cream over a gentle heat, adding a little extra stock or water if necessary to make the juices into a thick pouring sauce.

5 Arrange the chicken on a plate, surrounded by the creamy mushrooms. Garnish with the parsley sprigs and serve the chicken with the sauce and fresh green beans.

Chicken in Badacsonyi Wine

In Hungary, this recipe is made with a Balatan wine called *Badacsonyi Këkryalii* ("Blue Handled"), which has a full body and distinctive bouquet.

INGREDIENTS

Serves 4

50g/2oz/4 tbsp butter
4 spring onions, chopped
115g/4oz rindless smoked
   bacon, diced
2 bay leaves
1 tarragon sprig
1.5kg/3lb cornfed chicken
60ml/4 tbsp sweet sherry or mead
115g/4oz/scant 2 cups button
   mushrooms, sliced
300ml/½ pint/1¼ cups *Badacsonyi*
   or dry white wine
salt
tarragon and bay leaves,
   to garnish
fresh steamed rice, to serve

1 Heat the butter in a large heavy-based pan or flameproof casserole and sweat the spring onions for 1–1½ minutes. Add the bacon, bay leaves and the tarragon, stripping the leaves from the stem. Cook for a further 1 minute.

COOK'S TIP

Traditionally, this recipe also used a sweet drink with a honeyed caramel flavour called márc. If this is not available, replace it with sweet sherry or mead.

2 Add the whole chicken to the pan and pour in the sweet sherry or mead. Cook, covered, over a very low heat for 15 minutes.

3 Sprinkle the mushrooms into the pan and pour in the wine. Cook, covered, for a further 1 hour. Remove the lid, baste the chicken with the wine mixture and cook, uncovered, for a further 30 minutes, until almost all the liquid has evaporated.

4 Skim the cooking liquid remaining in the pan. Season to taste and remove the chicken, vegetables and bacon to a serving dish. Garnish with tarragon and bay leaves and serve with freshly cooked rice.

Roast Goose with Apples

Ganzebraten mit Apfeln symbolizes Christmas dinner in Germany. Here it is served with hazelnut- and honey-stuffed apples.

INGREDIENTS

Serves 6
115g/4oz/scant 1 cup raisins
finely grated rind and juice of 1 orange
25g/1oz/2 tbsp butter
1 onion, finely chopped
75g/3oz/¾ cup hazelnuts, chopped
175g/6oz/3 cups fresh white
   breadcrumbs
15ml/1 tbsp clear honey
15ml/1 tbsp chopped fresh marjoram
30ml/2 tbsp chopped fresh parsley
6 red eating apples
15ml/1 tbsp lemon juice
4.5–5kg/10–11lb oven-ready
   young goose
salt and freshly ground black pepper
fresh herbs, to garnish
orange wedges, red cabbage and green
   beans, to serve

1 Preheat the oven to 220°C/425°F/ Gas 7. Put the raisins in a bowl and pour over the orange juice. Melt the butter in a frying pan and then gently cook the onion for 5 minutes.

2 Add the chopped nuts to the pan and cook for a further 4–5 minutes, or until beginning to brown.

3 Add the cooked onion and nuts to the raisins with 50g/2oz/1 cup of the breadcrumbs, the orange rind, honey, herbs and seasoning. Mix well.

4 Wash the apples and remove the cores to leave a 2cm/¾ in hole. Using a sharp knife, make a shallow cut around the middle of each apple. Brush the cut and the cavity with the lemon juice to prevent it from browning.

5 Pack the centre of each apple with the nut and raisin stuffing.

6 Mix the remaining breadcrumbs into the stuffing and stuff the bird's tail end. Close with a small skewer.

7 Place the goose in a roasting tin, then prick the skin all over with a skewer. Roast for 30 minutes, then reduce the oven temperature to 180°C/350°F/Gas 4 and cook for a further 3 hours, pouring the excess fat out of the tin several times.

8 Arrange the apples around the goose and bake for 30–40 minutes, or until tender. Rest the goose in a warm place for 15 minutes, before carving. Garnish with fresh herbs, stuffed apples and orange wedges, with red cabbage and green beans.

COOK'S TIP

To test whether the goose is cooked, pierce the thigh with a thin skewer. The juice that runs out should be pale yellow. If it is tinged with pink, roast the goose for a further 10 minutes and test again.

FISH

*Indigenous central European freshwater fish include carp, pike, trout, bream
and wels, a type of catfish. A popular saltwater fish is cod. Fresh fish is often
baked or poached and served with sauces, such as the German recipe for Cod
in Mustard Sauce or the Czech recipe for Carp in Black Sauce. Many of
these recipes have remained unchanged for generations – such as Hungarian
Fish Sausages dating from the 17th century and German Blue Trout – and
are still the best way to appreciate the distinctive flavours of these fish.*

Baked Pike with Wild Mushrooms

Pike is a large family of fish found in the rivers of Europe. It has a good, fresh flavour and firm white flesh, making it perfect for baking in a creamy-paprika sauce with wild mushrooms and peppers.

INGREDIENTS

Serves 4–6

about 1.5kg/3lb whole pike
  or perch
115g/4oz/½ cup butter
115g/4oz/½ cup finely sliced onion
225g/8oz/3 cups wild mushrooms,
  roughly sliced
15ml/1 tbsp paprika
25ml/1½ tbsp flour
250ml/8fl oz/1 cup soured cream
15ml/1 tbsp finely chopped
  green pepper
salt and freshly ground black pepper

1 Preheat the oven to 190°C/375°F/ Gas 5. Clean, skin and fillet the fish and put the bones and skin in a large pan. Cover with cold water and bring to the boil. Reduce the heat, season and simmer for 30 minutes.

—— COOK'S TIP ——

Perch or any firm-fleshed white fish can be used instead of pike.

2 Meanwhile, butter a roasting tin, add the fillets and lightly season.

3 Melt the remaining butter in a pan and add the onion. Cook gently for 3–4 minutes, before adding the mushrooms. Cook for a further 2–3 minutes then sprinkle in the paprika.

4 Strain the fish stock, ladle out 250ml/8fl oz/1 cup and pour into the onion and mushrooms.

5 Blend the flour with the soured cream, stir into the pan, then pour over the fish. Bake for 30 minutes or until just tender. Sprinkle the green pepper over the top of the onion and mushroom mixture just before serving.

Carp in Black Sauce

This Czech dish is usually served on Christmas Eve. The carp is generally sold alive and then kept in fresh clean water – often in the bath – until required.

INGREDIENTS

Serves 4

50g/2oz/4 tbsp butter
1 onion, sliced
2 carrots, diced
2 small parsnips, diced
¼ small celeriac, diced
juice of 1 lemon
50ml/2fl oz/¼ cup red wine vinegar
175ml/6fl oz/¾ cup dark ale
8 whole black peppercorns
2.5ml/½ tsp allspice
1 bay leaf
5ml/1 tsp chopped fresh thyme
2cm/¾in piece of root ginger, peeled and grated
1 strip of lemon peel
3 slices of dark pumpernickel bread, processed into crumbs
30ml/2 tbsp flour
15ml/1 tbsp sugar
40g/1½oz/⅓ cup raisins
6 ready-to-eat prunes
30ml/2 tbsp hazelnuts and almonds, roughly chopped
4 thick carp or sea bream steaks
salt and freshly ground black pepper
fresh snipped chives, to garnish
dumplings and fresh bread, to serve

1 Melt half of the butter in a flame-proof casserole. Add the onion and cook for 2–3 minutes, then stir in the carrots, parsnips and celeriac. Cook for a further 5 minutes.

2 Stir in the lemon juice, red wine vinegar and dark ale. Pour in just enough water to cover.

3 Place the peppercorns, allspice, bay leaf, thyme, ginger, lemon peel and a little seasoning, in a bowl. Stir in the breadcrumbs, mix well and add to the vegetables. Simmer for 15 minutes.

4 Meanwhile, melt the remaining butter in a small pan and sprinkle in the flour. Cook gently for 1–2 minutes before adding the sugar. Cook for a further 2–3 minutes or until the sugar caramelizes.

5 Gradually ladle all of the stock from the casserole into the flour mixture; stir well then pour this back into the vegetable mixture. Add the raisins, prunes and nuts, and seasoning.

6 Place the fish steaks on top of the vegetables and cook for 12–15 minutes. To serve, arrange the fish on dishes, strain the vegetables, nuts and fruit and place them around the fish. Reduce the sauce by boiling quickly. Garnish with snipped chives and serve with dumplings and fresh bread.

Fish Goulash

This wholesome meal is a cross between a stew and a soup. It is traditionally served with a hot cherry pepper in the centre of the serving plate and the goulash ladled over it.

INGREDIENTS

Serves 6

2kg/4¹/₂lb mixed fish
4 large onions, sliced
2 garlic cloves, crushed
¹/₂ small celeriac, diced
handful of parsley stalks or
  cleaned roots
30ml/2 tbsp paprika
1 green pepper, seeded and sliced
5–10ml/1–2 tsp tomato purée
salt
90ml/6 tbsp soured cream and
  3 cherry peppers (optional),
  to serve

1 Skin and fillet the fish and cut the flesh into chunks. Put all the fish heads, skin and bones into a large pan, together with the onions, garlic, celeriac, parsley stalks, paprika and salt. Cover with water and bring to the boil. Reduce the heat and simmer for 1¹/₄ –1¹/₂ hours. Strain the stock.

2 Place the fish and green pepper in a large frying pan and pour over the stock. Blend the tomato purée with a little stock and pour it into the pan.

3 Heat gently but do not stir, or the fish will break up. Cook for just 10–12 minutes but do not boil. Season to taste. Ladle into warmed deep plates or bowls and top with a generous spoonful of soured cream and a halved cherry pepper, if liked.

Fish Sausages

This recipe has featured in many Hungarian cookbooks since the 17th century.

INGREDIENTS

Serves 3–4

375g/13oz fish fillets, such as perch,
  pike, carp, cod, skinned
1 white bread roll
75ml/5 tbsp milk
25ml/1¹/₂ tbsp chopped fresh flat
  leaf parsley
2 eggs, well beaten
50g/2oz/¹/₂ cup plain flour
50g/2oz/1 cup fine fresh
  white breadcrumbs
oil, for shallow frying
salt and freshly ground black pepper
deep fried sprigs of parsley and lemon
  wedges, sprinkled with paprika,
  to serve

1 Mince or process the fish coarsely in a food processor or blender. Soak the roll in the milk for about 10 minutes, then squeeze it out. Mix the fish and bread together before adding the chopped parsley, one of the eggs and seasoning.

2 Using your fingers, shape the mixture into 10cm/4in long sausages, about 2.5cm/1in thick.

3 Carefully roll the fish "sausages" into the flour, then in the remaining egg and then lastly in the breadcrumbs.

4 Heat the oil in a pan then slowly cook the "sausages" until golden brown all over. Drain well on crumpled kitchen paper. Garnish with deep fried parsley sprigs and lemon wedges sprinkled with paprika.

Halibut Cooked Under a Mountain of Cream

Halibut steaks are lightly cooked with bacon and wine, smothered in cream sauce and flash-grilled.

Ingredients

Serves 4

1 small onion, chopped
4 parsley sprigs
1 bay leaf
6 whole black peppercorns
150ml/¼ pint/⅔ cup white wine
8 lean streaky bacon rashers, rinded
4 halibut steaks, about 900g/2lb
   in total
10ml/2 tsp plain flour
15g/½oz/1 tbsp butter, softened
1.5ml/¼ tsp salt
pinch of paprika
120ml/4fl oz/½ cup double cream,
   lightly whipped
25g/1oz/⅓ cup grated Parmesan
sage leaves, to garnish
Parmesan, paprika and lemon, to serve

1 Preheat the oven to 180°C/350°F/ Gas 4. Put the onion, parsley, bay leaf, whole black peppercorns and wine in a small pan. Bring to the boil, then cover and simmer for 15 minutes. Leave to cool.

2 Cook the bacon rashers in a non-stick frying pan until lightly browned. Arrange the fish steaks in a greased shallow ovenproof dish. Place the bacon on top.

3 Strain the infused wine into the dish through a sieve, discarding the cooked onion and herbs. Bake in the oven for 12–15 minutes, or until the fish is just cooked.

4 Remove and reserve the bacon rashers. Strain the fish cooking liquid into a pan, again through a sieve, and bring to the boil.

5 Blend the flour and the butter to a paste in a small bowl. Whisk into the pan of stock and simmer for 3–4 minutes. Season with salt and paprika. Fold the cream into the sauce.

6 Transfer the fish to serving plates. Pour the sauce over the fish and sprinkle with the grated Parmesan. Place under a preheated medium grill for 3–4 minutes, or until lightly browned. Serve straight away, sprinkled with the reserved bacon cut into strips and garnished with sage leaves. Serve with extra Parmesan, paprika and lemon slices.

Baked Carp

Indigenous to the area, carp is a major ingredient in Hungarian cooking. It has a sweet, firm flesh that tastes wonderful when baked with bacon and bay leaves.

INGREDIENTS

Serves 4–6

450g/1lb old potatoes, scrubbed
115g/4oz rindless smoked bacon
about 900g/2lb whole carp, skinned,
    filleted and cut into 7.5cm/3in pieces
8–12 bay leaves
15ml/1 tbsp lard
1 onion, thinly sliced
15ml/1 tbsp paprika
1 large tomato, sliced
2 green peppers, seeded and sliced
40g/1½oz/3 tbsp butter, melted
150ml/¼ pint/⅔ cup soured cream
salt
bay leaves, to garnish

1 Preheat the oven to 190°C/375°F/ Gas 5. Boil the potatoes in their skins in a pan of boiling salted water for 15–20 minutes. Drain the potatoes and slice them.

2 Meanwhile, cut the bacon into strips. Make incisions in the fillets and push in the bacon and bay leaves.

COOK'S TIP

Pungent, salty bacon is a great partner for white fish: this is a combination found in many European cuisines.

3 Put the potatoes in a large well-buttered casserole. Add salt.

4 Melt the lard and fry the onion slices for 1–2 minutes. Stir in the paprika. Arrange the onion on the potato slices.

5 Place a layer of tomato and peppers on top of the onion then add the fish and a little salt.

6 Pour the melted butter over the fish. Bake in the oven for 30 minutes. Pour over the soured cream and cook for a further 15 minutes. Serve garnished with bay leaves.

Haddock with Mustard

The secret of this simple Czech recipe is to poach the fish in homemade stock.

INGREDIENTS

Serves 4
900g/2lb piece of haddock or carp,
  cut into 4 pieces
20ml/4 tsp ready-made
  English mustard
50g/2oz/4 tbsp butter
1 onion, sliced
15ml/1 tbsp cornflour
5–10ml/1–2 tsp lemon juice
salt
sprigs of tarragon, to garnish

For the stock
475ml/16fl oz/2 cups water
115g/4oz cabbage leaves, chopped
1 bay leaf
5 whole white peppercorns
5 allspice berries

1 To make the stock, bring the water, cabbage, bay leaf, peppercorns and allspice to the boil, then simmer for 20 minutes. Strain well.

--- COOK'S TIP ---

Home-made vegetable stock, made by boiling vegetables and aromatic herbs, is far superior in flavour to commercial stock cubes. Stock freezes well so can be made in large quantities and frozen in handy-size portions ready to use as required. Keep only for 3–4 months in the freezer.

2 Sprinkle the fish with salt then spread the mustard over the top.

3 Melt the butter in a frying pan and cook the sliced onion for 2 minutes until soft, then add the fish and brown the flesh well. Add the strained stock and simmer very gently for 10–15 minutes, until tender.

4 Transfer the fish to warm serving plates using a fish slice.

5 Mix the cornflour with the lemon juice and a little water to make a paste and add to the pan. Bring to the boil, then simmer for 5 minutes. Season to taste. Pour the sauce over the fish and garnish with sprigs of tarragon.

Pike in Horseradish Cream

The firm flesh of pike makes it ideally suited to poaching. The creamy sauce is wonderfully offset by the spiciness of the fresh horseradish.

INGREDIENTS

Serves 6

1 litre/1³/₄ pints/4 cups water
1 large onion, finely sliced
2 celery sticks, finely diced
2 carrots, thinly sliced
1 parsnip, finely diced
l0ml/2 tsp salt
6 whole peppercorns
fresh herb bouquet garni
about 1.5–1.75kg/3–4lb whole pike
15ml/1 tbsp plain flour
175ml/6fl oz/³/₄ cup soured cream
40g/l¹/₂oz/3 tbsp unsalted butter,
  melted
50–75g/2–3oz/¹/₂–³/₄ cup grated
  fresh horseradish
freshly ground mixed peppercorns
fennel flowers and sprigs of fennel,
  to garnish
green cabbage, to serve

1 Pour the water into a large pan or fish kettle, sprinkle in the onion, celery, carrots, parsnip, salt and whole peppercorns. Add the bouquet garni and simmer for 45 minutes.

COOK'S TIP

If fresh horseradish is unavailable use 30ml/2 tbsp hot bottled horseradish sauce.

2 Place the fish in the pan or fish kettle, cover and poach very slowly for 20 minutes, or until it is just cooked.

3 Using a fish slice remove the fish, cut into portions and keep warm. Strain the fish stock through a sieve into a large pan and simmer to reduce the liquid by about half. Blend the flour in a bowl with the soured cream and stir in the melted butter.

4 When the stock is reduced, whisk in the soured cream mixture, grated horseradish and freshly ground pepper. Bring to the boil then simmer for 2–3 minutes. Pour the sauce over the fish. Garnish with fennel flowers and sprigs of fennel and serve on a bed of green cabbage.

Blue Trout

The blue sheen of *Blaue Forelle* is a German speciality and is easily achieved by first scalding the fish and then fanning to cool it. Traditionally the fish was left to cool in a breeze or draught.

INGREDIENTS

Serves 4
4 trout, about 175g/6oz each
5ml/1 tsp salt
600ml/1 pint/2½ cups white
   wine vinegar
1 onion, sliced
2 bay leaves
6 whole black peppercorns
bay leaves and lemon slices, to garnish
115g/4oz/½ cup melted butter,
   creamed horseradish sauce and green
   beans, to serve

1 Preheat the oven to 180°C/350°F/ Gas 4. Rub both sides of the trout with salt and place in a non-aluminium roasting tin or fish kettle.

2 Bring the vinegar to the boil and slowly pour over the trout. Fan the fish as it cools or leave to stand in a draught for 5 minutes.

3 Bring the vinegar back to the boil, then add the sliced onion, bay leaves and peppercorns.

4 Cover the tin with foil and cook in the oven for 30 minutes, or until the fish is cooked. Transfer the fish to warmed serving dishes, garnish with bay leaves and lemon slices, and serve with melted butter, creamed horseradish sauce and green beans.

Baked Salmon

This Czech recipe uses freshwater fish such as salmon or trout but saltwater fish such as mackerel can also be used. It is a very simple but tasty meal as the fish cooks in its own juices.

INGREDIENTS

Serves 6
1.75kg/4lb whole salmon
115g/4oz/½ cup butter, melted
2.5–5ml/½–1 tsp caraway seeds
45ml/3 tbsp lemon juice
salt and freshly ground pepper
sprigs of flat leaf parsley and lemon
   wedges, to garnish

--- COOK'S TIP ---

Take care when cutting the fish: dip your fingers into a little salt to help you to grip the fish better.

1 Preheat the oven to 180°C/350°F/ Gas 4. Using a sharp knife, cut the fish in half lengthways.

2 Place the salmon, skin side down, in a lightly greased roasting tin and brush with the melted butter. Season, sprinkle over the caraway seeds and then the lemon juice.

3 Bake the salmon in the oven, loosely covered with foil, for 25 minutes or until the flesh flakes easily.

4 Transfer the fish to a serving plate. Garnish with flat leaf parsley and lemon wedges. Serve hot or cold.

Marinated Fish

With a number of tart flavours, this is a strong, zesty marinade.

INGREDIENTS

Serves 6–8
1.75kg/4lb tuna, carp or pike steaks
75g/3oz/6 tbsp butter, melted
50ml/2fl oz/¼ cup dry sherry
salt and freshly ground black pepper

For the marinade
400ml/14fl oz/1²/₃ cups water
150ml/¼ pint/²/₃ cup wine vinegar
150ml/¼ pint/²/₃ cup good fish stock
1 onion, thinly sliced
6 white peppercorns
2.5ml/½ tsp allspice
2 cloves
1 bay leaf
25ml/1½ tbsp bottled capers, drained
   and chopped
2 dill pickles, diced
120ml/4fl oz/½ cup olive oil
salad, dill pickles and bread, to serve

1 Preheat the oven to 180°C/350°F/ Gas 4. Put the fish steaks into an ovenproof dish and brush with the butter. Sprinkle over the sherry. Season well and bake for 20–25 minutes, or until just tender. Leave to cool.

—————— COOK'S TIP ——————

Use plump fillets of fish if tuna steaks are not available.

2 Meanwhile, boil the water, vinegar, fish stock, onion, spices and bay leaf together in a pan for 20 minutes. Leave to cool before adding the capers, dill pickle and olive oil.

3 Once the fish steaks have cooled pour over the marinade.

4 Cover the dish with clear film and leave to marinate the fish for 24 hours in the refrigerator, basting occasionally. Serve with a green salad, dill pickles and slices of pumpernickel or rye bread.

Cod in Mustard Sauce

A firm, white-fleshed fish, cod is abundant in the North Sea and features in many German recipes. Reduced stock sauces, as in this dish, are tending to replace the heavier flour-based versions of former times.

INGREDIENTS

Serves 4
900g/2lb cod fillets
1 lemon
1 small onion, sliced
15g/½oz/¼ cup chopped fresh flat
   leaf parsley, whole stalks reserved
6 allspice berries
6 whole black peppercorns
1 clove
1 bay leaf
1.2 litres/2 pints/5 cups water
30ml/2 tbsp wholegrain mustard
75g/3oz/6 tbsp butter
salt and freshly ground black pepper
bay leaves, to garnish
boiled potatoes and carrots,
   to serve

1 Place the fish on a plate. Pare two thin strips of rind from the lemon, then squeeze the lemon for its juice. Sprinkle the juice over the fish.

2 Put the lemon rind in a large frying pan with the onion, the stalks from the parsley, the allspice, peppercorns, clove and bay leaf.

3 Pour in the water. Slowly bring to the boil, cover and simmer for 20 minutes. Add the fish, cover and cook *very* gently for 10 minutes.

4 Ladle 250ml/8fl oz/1 cup of the cooking liquid into a pan and simmer until reduced by half. Stir in the mustard.

5 Whisk the butter, a little at a time, into the reduced stock. Taste and season with salt and pepper, if needed.

6 Remove the fish from the stock and place on warmed serving dishes. Pour over a little sauce and serve the rest separately in a jug. Garnish with chopped parsley and bay leaves and serve with boiled potatoes and carrots.

VEGETABLES, GRAINS AND PASTA

Home-grown vegetables form part of the local economy in much of rural central Europe. Vegetables may be pickled to preserve them throughout the year or used fresh in many interesting ways. Potatoes form an important part of the diet – served hot, made into potato cakes or eaten cold in salads. More popular in southern Germany is a pasta dish called Spätzle. Dried beans and pulses can be served on their own or as part of a main meal to extend the protein in dishes, particularly in Czech and Hungarian cooking.

Potato Salad

Use either new or waxy potatoes for this classic East European salad, since they will hold their shape when cooked.

INGREDIENTS

Serves 6
750g/1½lb potatoes, scrubbed
45ml/3 tbsp olive oil
4 smoked streaky bacon rashers, rinded and chopped
10ml/2 tsp lemon juice
2 celery sticks, chopped
2 pickled sour cucumbers, diced
5ml/1 tsp Dusseldorf or German mustard
45ml/3 tbsp mayonnaise
30ml/2 tbsp snipped fresh chives
15ml/1 tbsp chopped fresh dill
salt and freshly ground pepper
fresh chives and dill,
   to garnish

1 Cook the potatoes in a pan of boiling salted water for 15 minutes, until just tender. Drain, allow to cool for 5 minutes, then slice thickly and set aside in a bowl.

—————— COOK'S TIP ——————

German mustard is typically dark with a medium heat and a slightly sweet flavour; it is an ideal accompaniment for sausages, ham and bacon.

2 Meanwhile, heat 15ml/1 tbsp of the oil in a frying pan and fry the bacon for 5 minutes, until crispy. Remove the bacon and set aside.

3 Stir the remaining oil and lemon juice into the pan then pour over the sliced warm potatoes. Add the celery, cucumber and half the bacon and mix well. Leave to cool.

4 Blend the mustard in a small bowl with the mayonnaise, herbs and a little seasoning. Add to the potatoes and toss well to coat. Spoon the potatoes into a serving dish and sprinkle with the remaining bacon. Garnish with the fresh herbs and serve with lettuce leaves.

Himmel und Erde

This dish from the Rhineland, whose name translates as "heaven and earth", combines apples "from heaven" and potatoes "from the earth", and is served with slices of black pudding and crisp onion rings.

INGREDIENTS

Serves 4

450g/1lb floury potatoes, peeled and quartered
350g/12oz cooking apples, cored, peeled and chopped
50g/2oz/4 tbsp butter
2 cloves
pinch of nutmeg
30ml/2 tbsp sunflower oil
350g/12oz *blutwurst* (black pudding), cut into 1cm/½ in slices
1 onion, sliced into rings
salt and freshly ground black pepper

1 Cook the potatoes in a pan of boiling salted water for 20 minutes, or until tender. Drain well.

2 Meanwhile, put the chopped apples and 15g/½ oz/1 tbsp of the butter in a small pan with the cloves. Cook gently for 10 minutes, until soft.

3 Discard the cloves then add the cooked apple to the potato with the remaining butter, nutmeg and a little salt and pepper.

4 Mash the mixture until smooth and creamy. Pile on to a serving plate and keep warm.

5 Meanwhile heat the oil in a frying pan and cook the black pudding for 5 minutes, or until crisp. Remove from the pan with a slotted spoon and arrange to one side of the purée.

6 Add the onion rings to the pan and fry for 12–15 minutes, until lightly browned and crispy. Pile on top of the purée and serve hot.

Kohlrabi Baked with Ham

Kohlrabi, which is German for "cabbage-turnip", is a member of the cabbage family with a delicate turnip-like taste. Kohlrabi may be purple or greenish-white and is delicious either raw, grated and sprinkled with salt, or cooked. The leaves can also be eaten – treat in the same way as spinach.

INGREDIENTS

Serves 4
50g/2oz/4 tbsp butter
4 kohlrabi, peeled and diced
225g/8oz thick ham, diced
30ml/2 tbsp chopped fresh parsley

For the sauce
3 egg yolks
250ml/8fl oz/1 cup double cream
30ml/2 tbsp plain flour
pinch of mace
salt and freshly ground black pepper

1 Preheat the oven to 180°C/350°F/ Gas 4. Melt the butter in a large frying pan and gently cook the kohlrabi for 8–10 minutes.

2 Arrange half of the kohlrabi in the bottom of a greased ovenproof dish. Top with the ham and parsley, and finish with the remaining kohlrabi.

COOK'S TIP

Choose the smallest kohlrabi you can find, as these will have the freshest flavour.

3 Beat the sauce ingredients together and pour over the kohlrabi and ham. Bake for 30–35 minutes or until golden brown, and serve hot.

Poached Celery

This simple but tasty way of presenting celery is one that can also be used for kohlrabi, cauliflower or leeks. Select a hard cheese with a medium to vintage flavour.

INGREDIENTS

Serves 4
4 celery hearts
25g/1oz/2 tbsp butter
250ml/8fl oz/1 cup dry white wine
salt and freshly ground black pepper
15ml/1 tbsp chopped fresh parsley, to garnish
grated cheese, to serve

1 Scrub the celery well and trim the ends. Cut the celery hearts in half lengthways.

2 Parboil or blanch the celery in a pan of boiling salted water for 5 minutes. Drain and rinse quickly under cold water. Gently pat dry with kitchen paper.

3 Melt the butter in a frying pan and gently cook the celery for 1–2 minutes. Pour in the wine and bring to the boil. Reduce the heat to a simmer.

4 Cook uncovered for 5 minutes or until just tender. Drain well. Sprinkle with parsley and black pepper and serve with grated cheese on top.

Somogy Beans

This recipe comes from Somogy in Hungary, but every region has its own speciality. Serve with roast chicken, if liked.

INGREDIENTS

Serves 6–8

450g/1lb/2½ cups dried white beans, such as haricots or white kidney beans, soaked overnight
1 bay leaf
225g/8oz piece of lean smoked rindless bacon
15g/½oz/1 tbsp lard
1 onion, very finely chopped
2 garlic cloves, crushed
15ml/1 tbsp plain flour
15–30ml/1–2 tbsp vinegar
generous pinch of sugar
120ml/4fl oz/½ cup soured cream
salt
sage leaves and paprika, to garnish

1 Drain the white beans already soaked overnight and rinse well.

2 Put the beans in a large pan with the bay leaf, bacon and water to cover. Cook for about 1¼–1½ hours, or until the beans are tender. Carefully remove the bacon and dice when cool. Drain the beans, reserving 120ml/4fl oz/½ cup of the cooking liquid. (It may be useful to reserve a little more than this, in case it is needed in Step 5.)

3 Melt the lard in a frying pan and stir in the onion, garlic and flour. Cook for 2–3 minutes, then slowly stir in the reserved cooking liquid. Stir well.

4 Return the beans to a pan. Add the bacon and onion and stir well.

5 Add the vinegar, sugar and soured cream to the pan. Season to taste. If required, add a little more cooking liquid if the bean mixture is too stiff. Garnish with sage leaves and paprika.

--- COOK'S TIP ---

Salt is added only at the end of this recipe, otherwise the beans become tough.

Lecsó

Like much of Eastern Europe, Hungary makes good use of its fresh produce. Many of its vegetable recipes are substantial, flavoursome dishes, intended to be eaten by themselves, as with this recipe, and not just as an accompaniment to meat, poultry or fish dishes.

Lecsó, in its most basic form of a thick tomato and onion purée, is also used as the basis for stews and other dishes.

INGREDIENTS

Serves 6–8
5 green peppers
30ml/2 tbsp vegetable oil or
   melted lard
1 onion, sliced
450g/1lb plum tomatoes, peeled
   and chopped
15ml/1 tbsp paprika
sugar and salt, to taste
grilled bacon strips, to garnish
crusty bread, to serve

1 Wipe the green peppers, remove the cores and seeds and slice the flesh into strips.

2 Heat the oil or lard. Add the onion and cook over a low heat for 5 minutes until just softened.

VARIATION

To vary this recipe add 115g/4oz/1 cup sliced salami, or some lightly scrambled eggs to the vegetables.

3 Add the strips of pepper and cook gently for 10 minutes.

4 Add the chopped tomatoes and paprika and season to taste with a little sugar and salt.

5 Simmer the ratatouille over a low heat for 20–25 minutes. Serve immediately, topped with the strips of grilled bacon and accompanied by crusty bread.

Hot Cheese Pastries

One of many recipes for cheese pastries, often served to guests with Hungarian wine.

INGREDIENTS

Makes about 30
400g/14oz packet puff pastry, thawed
1 large egg, beaten
115–150g/4–5oz Liptauer cheese (see Cook's Tip), finely crumbled

---
COOK'S TIP

Hungarian *liptauer* is a cheese spread made from a white sheep's milk cheese, *liptó*, spiced with paprika, salt and various other ingredients, such as onion, caraway seeds, mustard and capers. *Liptauer* has a heady, spicy flavour. If unavailable, use feta cheese or the Romanian *brinza* instead.

1 Preheat the oven to 200°C/400°F/Gas 6. Roll out the puff pastry on a lightly floured surface to a 30cm/12in long oblong about 5mm/¼in thick. Cut the pastry in half crossways.

2 Glaze the pastry with the beaten egg, sprinkle over the Liptauer cheese and push it lightly into the pastry. Cut the pastry into 15 × 2.5cm/6 × 1in strips.

3 Twist the pastry strips to form long spiral shapes. Place on a non-stick baking sheet and bake for 10–15 minutes, or until golden brown. Cool on a wire rack.

Bavarian Potato Dumplings

The cuisines of Germany and Central Europe are unimaginable without dumplings, consumed in all shapes and sizes. In this version, crunchy croûtons are placed in the centre.

INGREDIENTS

Serves 6
1.5kg/3lb potatoes, peeled
115g/4oz/⅔ cup semolina
115g/4oz/1 cup wholemeal flour
5ml/1 tsp salt
1.5ml/¼ tsp nutmeg
30ml/2 tbsp sunflower oil
2 thin white bread slices, crusts removed, cubed
1.5 litres/2½ pints/6¼ cups beef stock
freshly ground black pepper
chopped fresh flat leaf parsley, crispy bacon and onion slices, to garnish
melted butter, to serve

1 Cook the potatoes in a large pan of boiling salted water for 20 minutes, or until tender. Drain well, then mash and press through a sieve into a bowl. Add the semolina, flour, salt, a little pepper and the nutmeg and mix well.

2 Heat the oil in a frying pan and fry the cubes of bread until light golden brown. Drain the croûtons on kitchen paper.

3 Divide the potato mixture into 24 balls. Press a few of the fried croûtons firmly into each dumpling. Bring the stock to the boil in a large pan, add the dumplings and cook gently for 5 minutes, turning once.

4 Remove the dumplings with a slotted spoon and arrange on a warmed serving dish. Sprinkle with chopped parsley, crispy bacon and fried onion slices and serve with a jug of melted butter.

Spiced Red Cabbage

Cook this a day before serving. It is a perfect accompaniment to roast pork or game.

INGREDIENTS

Serves 6–8

3 thick rindless bacon rashers, diced
1 large onion, chopped
1 large red cabbage,
   evenly shredded
3 garlic cloves, crushed
15–25ml/1–1½ tbsp caraway seeds
120ml/4fl oz/½ cup water
2 firm, ripe pears, cored and
   evenly chopped
juice of 1 lemon
475ml/16fl oz/2 cups red wine
45ml/3 tbsp red wine vinegar
150g/5oz/scant ¾ cup clear honey
salt and freshly ground black pepper
caraway seeds and snipped fresh chives,
   to garnish

1 Dry fry the diced bacon in a pan over a gentle heat for 5–10 minutes, or until golden brown.

2 Stir in the onion and cook for 5 minutes or until pale golden.

3 Stir the cabbage, garlic, caraway seeds and the water into the pan. Cover and cook for 8–10 minutes.

4 Season well, then add the pears, lemon juice, red wine and vinegar. Cover and cook for 10–15 minutes. Stir in the honey.

5 If there is too much cooking liquid, remove the lid and allow it to reduce. The pears will have broken up in the pot, and the quantity reduced by one-third. Adjust the seasoning to taste and serve sprinkled with caraway seeds and snipped fresh chives.

Spätzle

This simple pasta dish comes from Swabia in south-west Germany, where it is more popular than potatoes and is served with many savoury dishes.

INGREDIENTS

Serves 4

350g/12oz/3 cups plain flour
2.5ml/½ tsp salt
2 eggs, beaten
about 200ml/7fl oz/scant 1 cup milk
    and water combined
15ml/1 tbsp sunflower oil
25g/1oz/2 tbsp butter, melted, plus
    diced bacon, poached celery hearts
    and freshly ground black pepper,
    to serve

1 Sift the flour and salt into a bowl and make a well in the centre. Add the eggs and enough of the milk and water to make a very soft dough.

2 Beat the dough until it develops bubbles, then stir in the oil and beat again. Bring a large pan of salted water to the boil.

3 Dampen a chopping board with water and place the dough on it. Shave off strips of the dough into the water using the broad side of a knife.

COOK'S TIP

Rinse the knife with water occasionally at Step 3, so that the dough does not stick to it. The faster you work at this stage, the lighter the texture of the *spätzle*.

4 Cook for 3 minutes, then remove the pieces with a slotted spoon. Rinse quickly in hot water and put in a warmed serving bowl and cover to keep warm. Repeat until all the dough has been used up.

5 Drizzle the melted butter over the top and serve immediately, topped with diced bacon. Serve with poached celery hearts, and sprinkled with freshly ground black pepper.

DESSERTS AND BAKES

Hungary, Germany and Austria are well known for an impressive range of cakes and desserts, an enviable excellence in the art of pastry-making and an accompanying café culture, which is famous world-wide. It is hard to know which is the greater delight – a slice of rich Black Forest Cherry Cake or melt-in-the-mouth Apple Strudel. Locally grown cherries, plums, apricots and nuts are typical ingredients, while apples appear widely in German desserts and, in particular, baked goods.

Black Forest Cherry Cake

Surprisingly, this famous and much-loved cake is a fairly recent invention. It comes from southern Germany where Kirsch is distilled.

INGREDIENTS

Serves 12

200g/7oz plain chocolate, broken into squares
115g/4oz/½ cup unsalted butter
3 eggs, separated
115g/4oz/½ cup soft dark brown sugar
45ml/3 tbsp Kirsch
75g/3oz/⅔ cup self-raising flour, sifted
50g/2oz/½ cup ground almonds

For the filling and topping

65g/2½ oz plain chocolate
65g/2½ oz plain chocolate-flavoured cake covering
45ml/3 tbsp Kirsch
425g/15oz can stoned black cherries, drained and juice reserved
600ml/1 pint/2½ cups double cream, lightly whipped
12 fresh cherries with stalks

1 Preheat the oven to 180°C/350°F/ Gas 4. Grease and base-line a deep 20cm/8in round cake tin with greased greaseproof paper. Melt the plain chocolate and butter in a heatproof bowl set over a pan of simmering water, stirring to mix. Remove from the heat and leave until barely warm.

2 Whisk the egg yolks and sugar in a bowl until very thick, then fold in the chocolate mixture and the Kirsch. Fold in the flour with the ground almonds. Whisk the egg whites in a grease-free bowl until stiff, then gently fold into the mixture.

3 Pour the mixture into the prepared cake tin and bake in the oven for 40 minutes, or until firm to the touch.

4 Allow the sponge to cool in the tin for 5 minutes, then turn out and cool on a wire rack. Use a long serrated knife to cut the cake horizontally into 3 even layers.

5 Meanwhile, make the chocolate curls. Melt the chocolate and chocolate cake covering in a heatproof bowl set over a pan of simmering water, as before. Cool for 5 minutes, then pour on to a board to set. Use a potato peeler to shave off thin curls.

6 Mix the Kirsch with 90ml/6tbsp of the reserved cherry juice. Place the bottom layer of sponge on a serving plate and sprinkle with 45ml/3 tbsp of the Kirsch syrup.

7 Spread one-third of the whipped cream over the sponge layer and scatter over half the cherries. Place the second layer of sponge on top and repeat with another third of the Kirsch syrup and cream and the remaining cherries. Place the final sponge layer on top and sprinkle the remaining Kirsch syrup over it.

8 Spread the remaining cream over the top of the cake. Sprinkle over the chocolate curls and top with the fresh cherries.

Sachertorte

There are many variations on this popular recipe for the most famous Viennese chocolate cake, claimed to be the creation of the Austrian Prince Metternich's chef, Franz Sacher, in the 1830s. Sachertorte is a rich chocolate cake, traditionally coated with a chocolate sugar syrup glaze. The icing used here is much simpler to make and the results are just as impressive.

INGREDIENTS

Serves 8–10

175g/6oz semi-sweet plain chocolate, broken into pieces
150g/5oz/10 tbsp unsalted butter
150g/5oz/³/₄ cup caster sugar
5ml/1 tsp vanilla essence
6 eggs, separated
200g/7oz/1³/₄ cups ground almonds
25g/1oz/4 tbsp cornflour, sifted
25g/1oz/¹/₄ cup plain flour, sifted
115g/4oz/scant ¹/₂ cup apricot jam

For the icing

225g/8oz plain chocolate, broken into pieces
250ml/8fl oz/1 cup double cream
50g/2oz milk chocolate, broken into pieces

1 Preheat the oven to 180°C/350°F/Gas 4. Grease and line a 23cm/9in cake tin. Place the plain chocolate in a heatproof bowl set over a small pan of gently simmering water. Heat gently for 3–5 minutes, or until the chocolate melts. Remove the bowl from the heat and stir until the chocolate is smooth. Cool slightly.

2 Cream the butter in a bowl until softened, then gradually beat in half the sugar until pale and fluffy. Gradually beat in the vanilla essence, egg yolks and melted chocolate until well mixed.

3 Whisk the egg whites in a grease-free bowl until stiff, then gradually whisk in the remaining sugar. Using a large metal spoon, carefully fold the egg whites into the cake, with alternate spoonfuls of the ground almonds, cornflour and plain flour.

4 Pour the mixture into the prepared cake tin and level the surface. Cook in the preheated oven for 1–1¹/₄ hours, or until a skewer inserted into the centre comes out clean. Remove the cake from the oven and leave to cool completely in the tin.

5 When cold, transfer the cake to a wire rack and carefully peel off the lining paper.

6 Place the jam in a small pan, heat gently until boiling then sieve. Brush over the top and sides of the cake. Leave to cool completely.

7 Melt the chocolate for the icing in a heatproof bowl set over a pan of gently simmering water, as before. Beat the chocolate once melted. Cool slightly then add the cream.

8 Carefully pour the plain chocolate combined with the cream over the cake, shaking the cake gently to ensure the chocolate icing is evenly spread. Leave the surface smooth or swirl the icing slightly using the back of a palette knife. Carefully transfer the cake to a serving plate and leave to cool.

9 Place the milk chocolate in a small heatproof bowl over simmering water, as before, and heat gently for 3 minutes, or until melted. Remove from the heat and stir until smooth. Spoon the melted chocolate into a piping bag fitted with a small writing nozzle and carefully pipe the word "Sacher" across the top of the cake. Leave to cool.

Apple Strudel

This classic recipe is usually made with strudel dough, but filo pastry makes a good shortcut.

INGREDIENTS

Serves 8–10

500g/1¼lb packet large sheets of filo
  pastry, thawed if frozen
115g/4oz/½ cup unsalted butter,
  melted
icing sugar, for dredging
cream, to serve

For the filling

1kg/2¼lb apples, cored, peeled
  and sliced
115g/4oz/2 cups fresh breadcrumbs
50g/2oz/4 tbsp unsalted butter, melted
150g/5oz/¾ cup sugar
5ml/1 tsp cinnamon
75g/3oz/generous ½ cup raisins
finely grated rind of 1 lemon

1 Preheat the oven to 180°C/350°F/ Gas 4. For the filling, place the sliced apples in a bowl. Stir in the breadcrumbs, butter, sugar, cinnamon, raisins and grated lemon rind.

2 Lay 1 or 2 sheets of pastry on a floured surface and brush with melted butter. Place another 1 or 2 sheets on top, and continue until there are 4–5 layers in all.

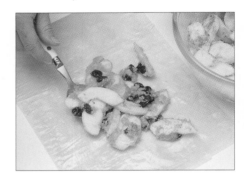

3 Put the apple on the pastry, with a 2.5cm/1in border all around.

4 Fold in the two shorter sides to enclose the filling, then roll up like a Swiss roll. Place the strudel on a lightly buttered baking sheet.

5 Brush the pastry with the remaining butter. Bake for 30–40 minutes or until golden brown. Leave to cool before dusting with icing sugar. Serve in thick diagonal slices.

Linzertorte

This sweet recipe was named not, as is commonly thought, after the town of Linz, but after Linzer, chef to the Archduke Charles, victor over Napoleon at Aspern in 1809.

INGREDIENTS

Serves 8–10

200g/7oz/scant 1 cup butter
  or margarine
200g/7oz/1 cup caster sugar
3 eggs, beaten
1 egg yolk
2.5ml/½ tsp cinnamon
grated rind of ½ lemon
115g/4oz/2 cups fine sweet
  biscuit crumbs
150g/5oz/1¼ cups ground almonds
225g/8oz/2 cups plain flour, sifted
225g/8oz/¾ cup raspberry jam
1 egg yolk, for glazing
icing sugar, to decorate

1 Preheat the oven to 190°C/375°F/ Gas 5. Cream the butter or margarine and sugar together in a mixing bowl until light and creamy. Add the eggs and egg yolk slowly, beating all the time, before adding the cinnamon and the lemon rind.

2 Stir the biscuit crumbs and ground almonds into the mixture. Mix well together before adding the sifted flour. Knead the pastry mixture lightly, then wrap it in clear film and allow to chill for 30 minutes.

3 Roll out two-thirds of the pastry on a lightly floured surface and use to line a deep 25cm/10in loose-based flan tin. Smooth down the surface.

4 Spread the raspberry jam over the base of the pastry case. Roll out the remaining pastry into a long oblong. Cut this into strips and arrange in a lattice pattern over the jam.

5 Brush the pastry with the beaten egg yolk to glaze. Bake the flan for 35–50 minutes, or until golden brown. Leave to cool in the tin before turning out on to a wire rack. Serve warm or cold with custard and sift over a little icing sugar.

COOK'S TIP

Sieve an extra 60ml/4 tbsp warmed raspberry jam and brush over the tart when cold.

Dobos Torta

This well-known cake was first created by a chef called Jozep Dobos in the late 1880s. His famous delicacy was soon exported worldwide in his specially designed packaging. Other cooks failed to replicate this treat, so in 1906 Dobos Makers donated his recipe to the Budapest Pastry and Honey-bread Makers Guild.

INGREDIENTS

Serves 10–12
6 eggs, separated
150g/5oz/1¼ cups icing
    sugar, sifted
5ml/1 tsp vanilla sugar
130g/4½oz/generous 1 cup plain
    flour, sifted

For the filling
75g/3oz plain chocolate, broken
    into pieces
175g/6oz/¾ cup unsalted butter
130g/4½oz/generous 1 cup
    icing sugar
30ml/2 tbsp vanilla sugar
1 egg

For the caramel topping
150g/5oz/¾ cup sugar
30–45ml/2–3 tbsp water
10g/¼oz/½ tbsp butter, melted

1 Preheat the oven to 220°C/425°F/ Gas 7. Whisk the egg yolks and half the icing sugar together in a bowl until pale in colour, thick and creamy.

2 Whisk the egg whites in a grease-free bowl until stiff; whisk in half the remaining icing sugar until glossy, then fold in the vanilla sugar.

3 Fold the egg whites into the egg yolk mixture, alternating carefully with spoonfuls of the flour.

4 Line 4 baking sheets with parchment or greaseproof paper. Draw a 23cm/9in circle on each piece of paper. Lightly grease the paper and dust with flour.

5 Spread the mixture evenly on the paper circles. Bake for 10 minutes, then leave to cool before layering and weighing them down with a board.

6 To make the filling, melt the chocolate in a small heatproof bowl set over a pan of gently simmering water. Stir until smooth.

7 Cream the butter and icing sugar together well in a bowl. Beat in the melted chocolate, vanilla sugar and egg.

8 Sandwich the 4 sponge circles together with the chocolate cream filling, then spread the remainder of the cream over the top and around the sides of the cake.

9 To make the caramel topping, put the sugar and water in a heavy-based pan and dissolve slowly over a very gentle heat. Add the butter.

10 When the sugar has dissolved, increase the heat and cook until the mixture turns golden brown. Quickly pour the caramel on to a greased baking sheet. Leave to set and shatter into shards when cold. Place the pieces of caramel on top of the cake, and cut it into slices to serve.

Baked Cheesecake with Kisel

This creamy cheesecake contrasts well with the flavour of fresh or stewed fruit, so why not try it with *kisel*? Originally a German recipe, the red-berry compôte became associated with Russia, where it was introduced by German governesses last century and is still a popular nursery food today.

INGREDIENTS

Serves 8–10
225g/8oz/2 cups plain flour
115g/4oz/½ cup butter
15g/½oz/1 tbsp caster sugar
finely grated rind of ½ lemon
1 egg, beaten
sprigs of mint, to decorate

For the filling
675g/1½lb/3 cups quark
4 eggs, separated
150g/5oz/¾ cup caster sugar
45ml/3 tbsp cornflour
150ml/¼ pint/⅔ cup soured cream
finely grated rind and juice of
　½ lemon
5ml/1 tsp vanilla essence

For the kisel
450g/1lb/4–4½ cups prepared red
　fruit, such as strawberries,
　raspberries, red currants, cherries
50g/2oz/¼ cup caster sugar
120ml/4fl oz/½ cup water
15ml/1 tbsp arrowroot

1 Begin by making the pastry for the cheesecake. Sift the flour into a bowl. Rub in the butter until the mixture resembles fine breadcrumbs. Stir in the caster sugar and lemon rind, then add the beaten egg and mix to a dough. Wrap in clear film and chill for at least 15 minutes.

2 Roll out the pastry on a lightly floured surface and use to line the base and sides of a 25cm/10in loose-bottomed cake tin. Chill for 1 hour.

3 Put the quark for the filling in a fine sieve set over a bowl and leave to drain for 1 hour.

4 Preheat the oven to 200°C/400°F/ Gas 6. Prick the chilled pastry case base with a fork, fill it with crumpled foil and bake for 5 minutes. Remove the foil and bake for a further 5 minutes. Remove the pastry case from the oven and reduce the oven temperature to 180°C/350°F/Gas 4.

5 Put the drained quark in a bowl with the egg yolks and caster sugar and mix together. Blend the cornflour in a cup with a little soured cream, then add to the bowl with the remaining soured cream, the lemon rind and juice and vanilla essence. Mix well.

6 Whisk the egg whites in a greaseproof bowl until stiff, then fold into the quark mixture, one-third at a time. Pour the filling into the pastry case and bake for 1–1¼ hours, until golden and firm. Turn off the oven and leave the door ajar. Let the cheesecake cool, then chill for 2 hours.

7 To make the kisel, put the prepared fruit, caster sugar and water into a pan and cook over a low heat until the sugar dissolves and the juices run. Remove the fruit with a slotted spoon and set aside.

8 Blend the arrowroot in a cup with a little cold water, stir into the fruit juices in the pan and bring to the boil, stirring all the time. Return the fruit to the pan and allow to cool, before serving it with the well-chilled cheesecake, decorated with sprigs of mint.

Apple Pancakes

These much-loved pancakes are filled with cinnamon-spiced caramelized apples.

INGREDIENTS

Serves 6
115g/4oz/1 cup plain flour
pinch of salt
2 eggs, beaten
175ml/6fl oz ¾ cup milk
120ml/4fl oz/½ cup water
25g/1oz/2 tbsp butter, melted
sunflower oil, for frying
cinnamon sugar or icing sugar and
    lemon wedges, to serve (optional)

For the filling

75g/3oz/6 tbsp butter
1.5kg/3lb eating apples, cored, peeled
    and sliced
50g/2oz/¼ cup caster sugar
5ml/1 tsp cinnamon

1 Melt the butter for the filling in a heavy-based frying pan. When the foam subsides, add the apple slices. Sprinkle a mixture of the sugar and cinnamon over the apples. Cook, stirring occasionally, until the apples are soft and golden brown. Set aside.

2 Sift the flour and salt into a mixing bowl and make a well in the middle. Add the eggs and gradually mix in the flour.

3 Slowly add the combined milk and the water, beating until smooth. Stir in the melted butter.

4 Heat 10ml/2 tsp oil in a crêpe or small frying pan. Pour in about 30ml/2 tbsp of the batter, tipping the pan to coat the base evenly.

5 Cook the pancake until the underside is golden brown, then turn over and cook the other side. Slide on to a warm plate, cover with foil and set the plate over a pan of simmering water to keep warm. Repeat with the remaining batter mixture, until it is all used up.

6 Divide the apple filling among the pancakes and roll them up. Sprinkle with cinnamon sugar or a dusting of icing sugar, if liked. Serve with lemon wedges to squeeze over.

COOK'S TIP

These pancakes taste equally good filled with sliced pears instead of apples, or a mixture of both apples and pears.

Spicy Apple Cake

Hundreds of German cakes and desserts include this versatile fruit. This moist and spicy *apfelkuchen* can be found on the menu of *Konditoreien,* coffee and tea houses, everywhere.

INGREDIENTS

Serves 12

115g/4oz/1 cup plain flour
115g/4oz/1 cup wholemeal flour
10ml/2 tsp baking powder
5ml/1 tsp cinnamon
2.5ml/½ tsp mixed spice
225g/8oz cooking apple, cored, peeled and chopped
75g/3oz/6 tbsp butter
175g/6oz/generous ¾ cup soft light brown sugar
finely grated rind of 1 small orange
2 eggs, beaten
30ml/2 tbsp milk
whipped cream dusted with cinnamon, to serve

For the topping

4 eating apples, cored and thinly sliced
juice of ½ orange
10ml/2 tsp caster sugar
45ml/3 tbsp apricot jam, warmed and sieved

1 Preheat the oven to 180°C/350°F/ Gas 4. Grease and line a 23cm/9in round loose-bottomed cake tin. Sift the flours, baking powder and spices together in a bowl.

2 Toss the chopped cooking apple in 30ml/2 tbsp of the flour mixture.

3 Cream the butter, brown sugar and orange rind together until light and fluffy. Gradually beat in the eggs, then fold in the flour mixture, the chopped apple and the milk.

4 Spoon the mixture into the cake tin and level the surface.

5 For the topping, toss the apple slices in the orange juice and set them in overlapping circles on top of the cake mixture, pressing down lightly.

6 Sprinkle the caster sugar over the top and bake for 1–1¼ hours, or until risen and firm. Cover with foil if the apples brown too much.

7 Cool in the tin for 10 minutes, then remove to a wire rack. Glaze the apples with the sieved jam. Cut into wedges and serve with whipped cream, sprinkled with cinnamon.

Bavarian Cream

This light dessert is set in a fancy mould and then turned out to serve. Decorate with cream and chocolate leaves or serve simply with fresh fruit.

INGREDIENTS

Serves 6
1 vanilla pod
300ml/¹/₂ pint/1¹/₄ cups single cream
15ml/1 tbsp powdered gelatine
45ml/3 tbsp milk
5 egg yolks
50g/2oz/¹/₄ cup caster sugar
300ml/¹/₂ pint/1¹/₄ cups double cream
chocolate leaves and a sprinkling of
  cocoa powder, to decorate

COOK'S TIP

If preferred, use 5ml/1 tsp vanilla essence instead of the vanilla pod. Omit Step 1 and whisk the vanilla essence along with the egg yolks and sugar at Step 3.

1 Put the vanilla pod and single cream into a small pan. Slowly bring to the boil, then turn off the heat, cover and infuse for 30 minutes. Remove the pod – rinsed well and dried, it can be stored and used again.

2 Sprinkle the gelatine over the milk and leave to soften.

3 Lightly whisk the egg yolks and caster sugar together in a heatproof bowl. Bring the single cream almost to the boil again, then whisk into the egg mixture.

4 Set the bowl over a pan of barely simmering water and cook the custard, stirring, until it thickens enough to coat the back of a wooden spoon. Remove from the heat, add the soaked gelatine and stir until dissolved.

5 Strain the custard into a clean bowl. Cover with a piece of wet greaseproof paper, to prevent a skin forming and leave to cool.

6 Whip the double cream in a bowl until it just holds soft peaks, then fold it into the cooled custard.

7 Rinse individual moulds or a 1.2 litre/2 pint/5 cup ring or fancy mould with water. Pour in the cream mixture and chill for at least 4 hours, or until set.

8 To unmould the Bavarian cream, dip the mould right up to the rim in very hot water for about 5 seconds. Place a serving plate on top, then quickly invert the mould and remove. Decorate with chocolate leaves and a sprinkling of cocoa powder.

Plum Streusel Slices

In Saxony, in eastern Germany, cakes and fruit desserts are frequently made with this crumble or "streusel" topping. Here, plums are used as the filling in this *pflaumenstreusel*.

INGREDIENTS

Makes 14

225g/8oz/1⅓ cups plums, stoned
   and chopped
15ml/1 tbsp lemon juice
50g/2oz/¼ cup sugar
115g/4oz/½ cup butter, softened
50g/2oz/¼ cup caster sugar
1 egg yolk
150g/5oz/1¼ cups plain flour

For the topping

150g/5oz/1¼ cups plain flour
2.5ml/½ tsp baking powder
75g/3oz/6 tbsp butter, chilled
50g/2oz/¼ cup soft light
   brown sugar
50g/2oz/½ cup chopped hazelnuts

1 Preheat the oven to 180°C/350°F/ Gas 4. Grease and base-line a 20cm/8in square cake tin. Put the plums and lemon juice in a small pan and cook over a low heat for 5 minutes, until soft.

2 Add the sugar to the pan and cook gently until dissolved. Simmer for 3–4 minutes until very thick, stirring occasionally. Leave to cool.

3 Beat the butter and caster sugar together in a bowl until light and fluffy. Beat in the egg yolk, then mix in the flour to make a soft dough. Press the mixture into the base of the prepared cake tin. Bake for 15 minutes. Remove from the oven and spoon the cooked plums over the base.

4 Meanwhile, to make the topping, sift the flour and baking powder into a bowl. Rub in the butter until the mixture resembles breadcrumbs. Stir in the sugar and chopped nuts.

5 Sprinkle the topping mixture over the plums and press it down gently. Return the tin to the oven and bake for a further 30 minutes, or until the topping is lightly browned. Leave to cool for 15 minutes, then cut into slices. Remove from the tin when completely cold.

— COOK'S TIP —

Fresh apricots are a delicious alternative to plums in this recipe.

Layered Pancake Gâteau

Pancakes in Hungary were originally very basic food: made with only cornflour and water, and then cooked over an open fire. The relative absence of ovens accounts for today's great variety of pancake recipes– both sweet and savoury – in this part of the world. This unusual layered pancake gâteau is just one example of this tradition.

INGREDIENTS

Serves 6
5 eggs, separated
50g/2oz/¼ cup caster sugar
175ml/6fl oz/¾ cup milk
50g/2oz/½ cup self-raising flour, sifted
50g/2oz/4 tbsp unsalted butter, melted
175ml/6fl oz/¾ cup soured cream
sifted icing sugar, for dredging
lemon wedges, to serve

For the filling
3 eggs, separated
25g/1oz/¼ cup icing sugar, sifted
grated rind of 1 lemon
2.5ml/½ tsp vanilla sugar
115g/4oz/1 cup ground almonds

1 Preheat the oven to 200°C/400°F/ Gas 6. Grease and line a deep 20–23cm/8–9in springform cake tin. Whisk the egg yolks and caster sugar together in a bowl until thick and creamy, before whisking in the milk.

2 Whisk the egg whites in a grease-free bowl until stiff, then fold into the batter mixture, alternating with spoonfuls of the flour and half the melted butter.

3 Take a frying pan as near to the size of your prepared cake tin as possible, and lightly grease the pan with a little of the remaining melted butter. Tilt to cover the surface.

4 Tip one-quarter of the batter into the frying pan. Fry the thick pancake on each side until golden brown, then slide it into the prepared cake tin. Use up the batter to make 3 more pancakes in the same way and set them aside while you make the filling.

5 For the filling, whisk the egg yolks in a bowl with the icing sugar until thick and creamy. Stir in the grated lemon rind and the vanilla sugar.

6 Whisk the egg whites in a separate bowl, then fold them into the egg yolk mixture, before adding the ground almonds. Mix together well.

7 Spread one-third of the mixture on top of the first pancake.

8 Repeat twice more with the second and third pancakes, then top with the final pancake.

9 Spread the soured cream over the top and bake for 20–25 minutes, or until the top is pale golden brown.

10 Leave in the tin for 10 minutes before removing the lining paper. Serve warm, cut into wedges, liberally dusted with icing sugar and accompanied by lemon wedges.

Plum Dumplings

Sweet dumplings such as these are popular right across central Eastern Europe. The potato-based dumpling makes an interesting and unusual contrast to the juicy fruit filling.

INGREDIENTS

Serves 4

250g/9oz potatoes, peeled
75g/3oz/6 tbsp unsalted butter
1 egg, beaten
130g/4½ oz/generous 1 cup plain
    flour, sifted
16 plums
16 blanched whole almonds
45ml/3 tbsp granulated sugar
50g/2oz/scant 1 cup day-old
    breadcrumbs
40–50g/1½–2oz/⅓–½ cup icing
    sugar, sifted
2.5ml/½ tsp ground cinnamon

1 Boil the potatoes in a large pan until just cooked. Drain then mash them with 25g/1oz/2 tbsp of the butter. Leave to cool before adding the egg. Mix well then stir in the flour.

2 Knead the dough until soft, on a lightly floured surface. Cover with clear film and chill for 30 minutes.

> —— COOK'S TIP ——
>
> For added sweetness, serve with fromage frais.

3 Carefully ease the stone out of each plum by slitting the plums without cutting them in half. Once the stone is removed push an almond into each plum with about 2.5ml/½ tsp of the granulated sugar.

4 Divide the dough into 16 even balls. Roll out each dough ball on a very lightly floured surface to a thin round. Brush the edges of each dough circle with water and wrap around a plum. Seal the dough to enclose the fruit completely.

5 Bring a large pan of lightly salted water to the boil, add the dumplings and simmer for 10–12 minutes. When cooked remove them with a slotted spoon and drain well, then rinse in cold water quickly. Drain well again.

6 Meanwhile, fry the breadcrumbs in the remaining butter in a pan until golden brown then quickly roll the dumplings in the breadcrumbs. Dredge the dumplings liberally with a mixture of icing sugar and cinnamon and serve them hot.

Stuffed Baked Apples

This is a very simple and tasty Czech dish that may be eaten hot or cold.

INGREDIENTS

Serves 4

75g/3oz/generous ½ cup raisins
45ml/3 tbsp rum
4 cooking apples
75g/3oz/¾ cup toasted hazelnuts (see Cook's Tip)
50g/2oz/¼ cup white sugar
175ml/6 fl oz/¾ cup double cream
30ml/2 tbsp honey
sprigs of mint, to decorate
whipped cream, to serve

1 Soak the raisins in half the rum for at least 2–3 hours.

2 Preheat the oven to 200°C/400°F/ Gas 6. Wash the apples, remove the cores and score around the middle of each with a sharp knife.

3 Put the hazelnuts in a food processor or blender and grind coarsely. Add the sugar, then pour in the cream. Add the raisins and mix briefly.

4 Spoon the stuffing into the apples. Place in an ovenproof dish.

5 Blend together the honey and the remaining rum and pour over the apples. Bake for about 35–40 minutes, basting the apples occasionally during cooking. Serve either hot or well chilled, decorated with sprigs of mint, with sweetened, whipped cream.

COOK'S TIP

To toast hazelnuts, put them on a baking sheet and place under a preheated moderate grill. Toast until the nuts are pale golden, stirring all the time. When cool, rub the nuts in a clean dish towel and the skins will come off fairly easily.

Stewed Fruit

This recipe is good for using up odd or small quantities of fresh fruit. Serve the medley of fruit well chilled.

INGREDIENTS

Serves 6
115–175g/4–6oz/½–¾ cup sugar, depending on the tartness of the fruit
250ml/8fl oz/1 cup cold water
juice and strip of rind from ½ lemon
1 cinnamon stick, broken into two
900g/2lb prepared fruit, such as cored, peeled and sliced apples, pears, quince; stoned plums, peaches, apricots; trimmed gooseberries; cranberries, blueberries, strawberries
30ml/2 tbsp arrowroot
caster sugar and cream (optional), to serve

1 Put the sugar and water into a stainless steel pan and bring to the boil. Add the lemon juice and rind and the two pieces of cinnamon stick. Cook for 1 minute.

2 Add the prepared fruit to the pan and cook for 2–3 minutes only. Remove the fruit and cinnamon stick with a slotted spoon.

3 Blend the arrowroot with a little cold water, stir into the fruit juices and bring to the boil. Return the fruit to the saucepan and allow the fruit to cool before chilling. Discard the cinnamon stick if you wish.

4 Serve the fruit sprinkled with caster sugar, and with whipped cream, if liked.

Sweet Cheese Dumplings

The most famous cheese dumplings come from Czech countries, but they are popular elsewhere, as this Austrian version shows. Sweet and savoury versions combined together, such as this one here, are known as *mehlspeisen*.

INGREDIENTS

Serves 4–6
40g/1½ oz/3 tbsp unsalted butter
3 eggs, separated
450g/1lb/2 cups curd cheese
50g/2oz/⅓ cup semolina
15ml/1 tbsp double cream
15–30ml/1–2 tbsp plain flour
sifted icing sugar and sprigs of mint, to decorate

1 Cream the butter and beat in the egg yolks, one at a time. Stir in the curd cheese, semolina and cream. Mix well, cover and stand for 45 minutes.

2 Whisk the egg whites in a grease-free bowl until stiff, then carefully fold into the curd cheese mixture together with the flour.

3 Boil a very large pan of salted water. Scoop spoonfuls of mixture about the size of a plum and roll into ovals or balls with damp hands.

4 Drop the dumplings into the boiling water and simmer for about 6–7 minutes. Remove with a slotted spoon and drain well. Serve warm, dredged liberally with icing sugar and decorated with sprigs of mint.

Noodle Pudding with Cherries and Nuts

This is an unusual dessert but one that is very popular in the Czech Republic, and takes full advantage of the local fruits.

INGREDIENTS

Serves 6

900ml/1½ pints/3¾ cups milk
450g/1lb/4 cups medium-sized
  egg noodles
350g/12oz/1½ cups butter
90ml/6 tbsp sugar
7 egg yolks
7.5ml/1½ tsp vanilla essence
75g/3oz/¾ cup ground walnuts
675g/1½lb stoned fresh cherries
50g/2oz/¼ cup caster sugar
50ml/2 fl oz/¼ cup cherry brandy
  (optional)

1 Preheat the oven to 180°C/350°F/
Gas 4. Grease and base-line a
23–25cm/9–10in square cake tin.
Bring the milk to the boil in a large
pan and add the noodles. Reduce the
heat and cook until the noodles have
absorbed the milk, stirring all the time.
Carefully, stir the butter into the pan
and cool well.

2 Beat the sugar in a bowl with the
egg yolks and vanilla essence. Very
carefully add the ground walnuts to the
noodles, then stir the egg yolk mixture
into the noodles, too.

3 Spread one-third of the noodles in
the bottom of the prepared cake
tin and level the surface.

4 Top the noodles with half of the
cherries, sugar and cherry brandy,
if using. Add another layer of noodles,
followed by the remaining cherries,
sugar and cherry brandy. Finish with a
final layer of noodles, smoothing down
the surface, then place the tin in the
oven and bake for 40–45 minutes, until
golden brown.

Soufflé Omelette

This fluffy jam-filled omelette makes a substantial dessert for 1 person, or can be cut in half to serve 2 people.

INGREDIENTS

Serves 1–2

3 eggs, separated
30ml/2 tbsp single cream
10ml/2 tsp caster sugar
pinch of salt
15g/½oz/1 tbsp unsalted butter
45ml/3 tbsp good-quality cherry or
    plum jam
30ml/2 tbsp icing sugar

1 Put the egg yolks, cream and caster sugar in a bowl and whisk together with a fork. In a grease-free bowl, whisk the egg whites with the salt until stiff. Lightly fold the egg whites into the yolk mixture.

2 Melt the unsalted butter in a large omelette pan, until bubbling. Pour in the egg mixture, spreading it evenly. Cook over a medium heat for 2–3 minutes, or until the base of the omelette is lightly browned.

3 Place the pan under a preheated grill for 2–3 minutes, until the top is lightly browned and set. Remove the omelette from the heat.

4 Meanwhile, heat the jam in a small pan. Spread it over the omelette and fold it in half. Transfer to a serving plate. Thickly dust the top of the omelette with the icing sugar.

5 Heat 2 metal skewers on the hob until red hot. Use to scorch a lattice pattern on the omelette. Serve immediately.

Nut Squares

This light and delicious Czech recipe is good with coffee in the morning or served as a dessert.

INGREDIENTS

Makes about 24
225g/8oz/1 cup unsalted butter
225g/8oz/generous 1 cup caster sugar
3 egg yolks
175g/6oz/1½ cups plain flour, sifted
4 eggs, beaten
175g/6oz/1½ cups ground walnuts
20g/¾oz/scant ⅓ cup day-old white breadcrumbs
cocoa powder for sprinkling

For the topping
3 egg whites
150g/5oz/¾ cup caster sugar
115g/4oz/1 cup ground walnuts
75g/3oz/½ cup raisins, chopped
25g/1oz/¼ cup cocoa powder, sifted

1 Preheat the oven to 150°C/300°F/ Gas 2. Grease and line a 28 × 18 × 4cm/11 × 7 × 1½in Swiss roll tin.

2 Cream the butter and caster sugar together until pale and fluffy, then beat in the egg yolks.

3 Fold half the flour into the mixture, then beat in the whole eggs slowly before stirring in the remaining flour and the walnuts.

4 Sprinkle the prepared Swiss roll tin with the breadcrumbs before spooning in the walnut mixture. Level the mixture with a round-bladed knife. Bake for 30–35 minutes or until cooked and pale golden brown.

5 Meanwhile, make the topping. Whisk the egg whites in a grease-free bowl until stiff. Slowly whisk in the sugar until glossy, before folding in the walnuts, raisins and cocoa powder.

6 Spread the topping mixture over the cooked base and cook for a further 15 minutes. Leave to cool in the tin. When cold, peel away the lining paper. Cut into squares or fingers, and sprinkle with cocoa powder.

Lebkuchen

These sweet and spicy cakes, a speciality of Nuremberg in Bavaria, are traditionally baked at Christmas. In German, their name means "cake of life".

INGREDIENTS

Makes 20

115g/4oz/1 cup blanched almonds,
   finely chopped
50g/2oz/¹⁄₃ cup candied orange peel,
   finely chopped
finely grated rind of ½ lemon
3 cardamom pods
5ml/1 tsp cinnamon
1.5ml/¹⁄₄ tsp nutmeg
1.5ml/¹⁄₄ tsp ground cloves
2 eggs
115g/4oz/scant ³⁄₄ cup caster sugar
150g/5oz/1¹⁄₄ cups plain flour
2.5ml/½ tsp baking powder
rice paper (optional)

For the icing

½ egg white
75g/3oz/³⁄₄ cup icing sugar, sifted
5ml/1 tsp white rum

1 Preheat the oven to 180°C/350°F/ Gas 4. Set aside some of the almonds for sprinkling and put the remainder in a bowl with the candied orange and lemon rind.

3 Whisk the eggs and sugar in a mixing bowl until thick and foamy. Sift in the flour and baking powder, then gently fold into the eggs before adding to the nut and spice mixture.

5 Bake for 20 minutes, until golden. Allow to cool for a few minutes, then break off the surplus rice paper or remove the biscuits from the baking paper and cool on a wire rack.

2 Remove the black seeds from the cardamom pods and crush using a pestle and mortar. Add to the bowl with the cinnamon, nutmeg and cloves and mix well.

4 Spoon dessertspoons of the mixture on to sheets of rice paper, if using, or baking paper placed on baking sheets, allowing room for the mixture to spread. Sprinkle over the reserved almonds.

6 Put the egg white for the icing in a bowl and lightly whisk with a fork. Stir in a little of the icing sugar at a time, then add the rum. Drizzle over the *lebkuchen* and leave to set. Keep in a tin for 2 weeks before serving.

Stollen

Dating from the 12th century, and symbolizing the Holy Child wrapped in cloth, this traditional German Christmas cake is made from a rich yeast dough with marzipan and dried fruits.

INGREDIENTS

Serves 12
375g/13oz/3 cups strong white
   bread flour
pinch of salt
50g/2oz/¼ cup caster sugar
10ml/2 tsp easy-blend dried yeast
150ml/¼ pint/⅔ cup milk
115g/4oz/½ cup butter
1 egg, beaten
175g/6oz/1 cup mixed
   dried fruit
50g/2oz/¼ cup glacé cherries,
   quartered
50g/2oz/½ cup blanched almonds,
   chopped
finely grated rind of 1 lemon
225g/8oz/1 cup marzipan
icing sugar, for dredging

1 Sift the flour, salt and sugar. Stir in the yeast. Make a well in the centre. Over a low heat, gently melt the milk and butter. Cool, then mix with the egg into the sifted dry ingredients.

2 Turn out the dough on to a lightly floured surface and knead for 10 minutes, until smooth and elastic. Put in a clean bowl, cover with clear film and leave in a warm place to rise for about 1 hour, or until doubled in size.

3 On a lightly floured surface knead in the dried fruit, cherries, almonds and lemon rind.

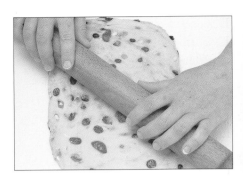

4 Roll out the dough to a rectangle, about 25 × 20cm/10 × 8in.

5 Roll the almond paste to a sausage, slightly shorter than the dough. Place on the dough in the middle. Enclose the paste in dough.

6 Put seam side down on a greased baking sheet. Cover with oiled clear film and leave in a warm place to rise for about 40 minutes, or until doubled in size. Preheat the oven to 190°C/375°F/Gas 5.

7 Bake the stollen for 30–35 minutes, or until golden and hollow sounding when tapped on the underside. Leave to cool on a wire rack. Serve thickly dusted with icing sugar.

Black Bread

Black bread is eaten throughout Eastern Europe. This German yeastless version has a dense texture similar to that of pumpernickel and is steamed rather than oven baked. Empty fruit cans are perfect for producing bread in the traditional round shape.

INGREDIENTS

Makes 2 loaves

50g/2oz/½ cup rye flour
40g/1½ oz/⅓ cup plain flour
4ml/¾ tsp baking powder
2.5ml/½ tsp salt
1.5ml/¼ tsp cinnamon
1.5ml/¼ tsp nutmeg
50g/2oz/⅓ cup fine semolina
60ml/4 tbsp black treacle
200ml/7fl oz/scant 1 cup cultured
 buttermilk
cherry jam, soured cream or crème
 fraîche and a sprinkling of ground
 allspice, to serve

1 Grease and line 2 × 400g/14oz fruit cans. Sift the flours, baking powder, salt and spices into a large bowl. Stir in the semolina.

COOK'S TIP

If you cannot get buttermilk, use ordinary milk instead, first soured with 5ml/1 tsp lemon juice.

2 Add the black treacle and buttermilk and mix thoroughly.

3 Divide the mixture between the 2 tins, then cover each with a double layer of greased pleated foil.

4 Place the cans on a trivet in a large pan and pour in enough hot water to come halfway up the sides. Cover tightly and steam for 2 hours, checking the water level occasionally.

5 Carefully remove the cans from the steamer. Turn the bread out on to a wire rack and cool completely. Wrap in foil and use within 1 week.

6 Serve the bread in slices, spread with cherry jam, topped with a spoonful of soured cream or crème fraîche and a sprinkling of allspice.

INDEX